First published March 2013

A catalogue record for this book is available from the British Library

ISBN 978 0 85733 380 3

Library of Congress catalog card no 2012953864

Published by Haynes Publishing in association with FireStep Publishing

Haynes Publishing,
Sparkford, Yeovil, Somerset BA22 7JJ, UK
Tel: 01963 442030
E-mail: sales@haynes.co.uk
Website: www.haynes.co.uk

FireStep Publishing,
Gemini House, 136-140 Old Shoreham Road, Brighton BN3 7BD
Tel: 0845 475 1945
E-mail: books@firesteppublishing.com
Website: www.firesteppublishing.com

Printed and bound in the UK by Gomer Press Limited,
Llandysul Enterprise Park, Llandysul, Ceredigion SA44 4JL

Publishing Directors	Ryan Gearing, Mark Hughes
Author	Stephanie Temple
Project Manager	Louise McIntyre
Design	Richard Parsons, Lee Parsons

Jacket illustrations

Front, top Members of the Race2Recovery team in front of their vehicles at the Tedworth House Recovery Centre (from left): Andrew 'Pav' Taylor, Phillip 'Barney' Gillespie, Marty Rae, Mark Zambon, Daniel 'Baz' Whittingham, Tim Read, Tom Neathway, John Winskill and Tony Harris.
Front, bottom The Peter Harrison Foundation funded Wildcat #445 'Joy', crewed by Major Matt O'Hare and Corporal Barney Gillespie, made history in 2013 by crossing the line of the world's toughest motorsport event, the Dakar Rally. **Back, clockwise from top left** Ben Gott and US Marine Mark Zambon charge out on the first day of their epic adventure; Corporal Tom Neathway of the Parachute Regiment in his position as navigator in the Orange Plant Wildcat, named in memory of Gordon Chapman; Captain Tony Harris of the Royal Regiment of Fusiliers working on his Wildcat in the sand dunes of Peru; the RatCat with Ben Gott and Mark Zambon demonstrates the awesome power of the Wildcat.

The publishers are grateful to the Race2Recovery team and the many amateur and professional photographers who kindly provided access to over 10,000 images for consideration. It has been possible to select only a fraction for this unique book and we wish to thank them wholeheartedly for their support.

The Race2Recovery team including: Tiff Hyde, Gareth Paterson, Mark Cullum, Ben Gott, Tim Read, Charles Sincock, Chris Astles, Chris Ratter, Marty Rae, Matt O'Hare, Rick Nixon, Tim Hare, Tony Harris

Other contributors:

Matt Austin
Lawrence Clift
James Arbuckle
Matt Cardy
James Tobin
David Dyson
Harvey Hook
Doug Scott
Tim Surman
David Shepherd
Robert W Kranz
Andrew Kentigern-Fox
Ryan Gearing
Emma Pascoe / Blacklimesphotography.co.uk
Marcel Vermeij / Rallymaniacs.nl
Fred Tigelaar / DDT Press
Franck Fife / Getty Images
Stringer / Reuters
Lenormand – Vargiolu – Flamand – Le Floch,
   Le Meur / DPPI
Crown Copyright / Sergeant Ian Forsyth RLC
Maindru
off-road-photography.co.uk

Special thanks to Gaucho Productions, the London-based film, television and PR company that was embedded with the team from the middle of 2012 to produce two TV documentary series: the first, *The Road to Dakar*, was shown on Eurosport over Christmas 2012; the second, following the team's exploits on the Dakar, was in post-production as this book closed for press. The Gaucho team, led by award-winning journalist and presenter Alistair Weaver, was also responsible for providing daily blogs and editorial reports from the Dakar. These featured in the *Sunday Times*, *The Independent*, *Autosport*, *Autocar*, *Octane*, *MSN*, *Edmunds* and *New York Daily News*, among others. Gaucho kindly donated its fee for providing content for this book to the Tedworth House Personal Recovery Centre.
www.gauchoproductions.com

RACE2RECOVERY

BEYOND INJURY, ACHIEVING THE EXTRAORDINARY

RACE2RECOVERY
CONTENTS

FOREWORD BY RICHARD HAMMOND	**4**
INTRODUCTION	**6**
THE TEAM	**18**
THE VEHICLES	**46**
THE TRAINING	**60**
FIRST OUTINGS	**76**
TUAREG RALLYE	**88**
THE BUILD-UP	**100**
DAKAR RALLY	**118**
EPILOGUE	**184**
ACKNOWLEDGEMENTS	**191**

We get to say a lot of stuff on *Top Gear*; some of it important, most of it ridiculous. But this… this was something special.

'You might remember the group of wounded soldiers we met on the show last year on a wet, Welsh hillside,' I announced during the news section of our show on 27 January 2013. Confident that most of our 350 million strong audience would indeed remember, I went on. 'They had decided to take on the toughest race in the world, the legendary Dakar.'

And at this point Jeremy interrupted to say that, yes, he remembered them and he remembered thinking they were nuts. I agreed, drew breath and then enjoyed possibly the most pleasurable moment of my two decades of blathering on the telly: 'Well, the race was over 8,500km long, it took two weeks and 30 per cent of the competitors didn't finish, but last Sunday, and this is incredible news, they did.'

Our studio audience whooped and hollered in the time-honoured fashion and we all applauded. But this was something special, something beyond the announcement of an F1 win or the launch of a new Ferrari. This was, well it was just that, beyond…

And I know that as soldiers, the guys won't take the piss if I tell you that I had a lump in my throat and a damp eye when I said it – in fact, they might actually stop taking the piss for a moment or two. Soldiers are like that: despite the hardships, the physical and mental strain, or I don't know, maybe partly because of it, they're human, more human perhaps than most, and they know it's OK sometimes to show it when you're moved by something. And I, along with the rest of the team on *Top Gear* and countless millions watching, was genuinely moved that this rag-tag bunch of variously battered and wounded soldiers could have the nerve, the confidence, the gumption, the sheer bloody-mindedness not only to take on a race that tests the nerve, strength and skill of the most experienced rally teams in the world, but to go through with it and finish it.

I'd say that their story is told in this book. But it isn't, not in full. Because their stories already contain enough epics to fill many, many more lives and, most importantly, they're not done yet. This is what they're like. They got shot or blown up, or maybe both, and they still forged on and did what you'll read about them doing in here. So what the hell will they do next? I for one look forward to seeing it.

Inspirational is an over-used word, especially in book forewords. But I think I can be excused its use here, because that is exactly what these men and women are. The quickest way to get the point is to read what one of the lads, Tony – you'll read about him – tweeted when setting off on yet another gruelling training mission. 'I used to worry about packing enough socks, now I have to think about packing enough legs.'

Enough said. Read on…

Richard Hammond
BBC *Top Gear*

'Our studio audience whooped and hollered in the time-honoured fashion… But this was something special, something beyond the announcement of an F1 win or the launch of a new Ferrari.'

Richard Hammond, BBC *Top Gear*

'Injury or disability needn't stop you from realising your dreams. You just have to go about things in a slightly different way!'

Captain Tony Harris

RACE2RECOVERY
ORIGINS

In 2010, Captain Tony Harris of the Royal Regiment of Fusiliers was recovering at the Headley Court rehabilitation centre in Surrey after having his left leg amputated below the knee following the explosion of an IED (Improvised Explosive Device) under his Jackal armoured vehicle in Helmand province, Afghanistan, the previous year. Inspired by two friends who were the brains behind the Row2Recovery challenge, Tony began to think about another endeavour...

Tony talked it over with his friend Tom Neathway, a corporal in the Parachute Regiment who'd lost his left arm and both legs above the knee after triggering a booby-trapped sandbag in Helmand province in 2008. They mulled over the possibilities and the idea of rallying came up. But their ambitions were much greater than simply taking part in a rally: both agreed that if they were going to do something like that they might as well do it properly and attempt the toughest rally in the world – the Dakar.

'In January 2011 I sent some emails out on the Help for Heroes Band of Brothers network,' explained Tony. 'I received lots of replies and one was from Pav [Andrew Taylor]. It really snowballed from there – the interest was astounding. I got Matt [O'Hare] involved as he's one of my best mates and I trust him with my life. Pav then had Barney [Phillip Gillespie] come on board and the rest, as they say, is history.'

And that was how Race2Recovery was born.

← Tony Harris laughs with the press at the pre-Dakar launch at Tedworth House in November 2012

'Their story is truly the stuff of legend. Supporters can share their inspirational journey and their expression of motivation, determination and bravery.'

Patron
Ben Collins
Top Gear's The Stig

RACE2RECOVERY
LIFE AFTER INJURY

Injury from an IED can change the life of someone who is attacked in this way to an unimaginable degree. The journey to the other side is never easy, but most wounded soldiers discover that life is still well worth living. Race2Recovery aims to champion the astonishing achievements of people with disabilities, and in doing so inspire others with life-altering injuries to realise their potential.

'Injury or disability needn't stop you realising your dreams. You just have to go about things in a slightly different way!' according to Tony Harris.

It only takes a few seconds for a soldier's life to change forever in a war zone. The number of British service personnel undergoing amputations since the war in Afghanistan began has reached around 250 to date. The period from 2008 and 2010 was particularly severe, when the rate of injuries sustained from IEDs more than doubled, though thankfully the figures have fallen since then. In the worst year, 2010, 76 soldiers required amputations and 37 of these suffered multiple amputations.

Inspired by the Row2Recovery campaign, which saw injured service personnel complete a 3,000-mile transatlantic row in January 2012, Race2Recovery has adopted the same values: determination, honour, camaraderie and inspiring others while always focusing on the principal aims of raising money and awareness of both the physical and mental scars these soldiers will bear for the rest of their lives.

It's not just the soldiers who have to come to terms with what has happened to them – family members also have to deal with the debilitating after-effects. Whether it's nightmares, flashbacks or depression, or even all of these, parents, partners and siblings can all struggle and need somewhere to turn to for help.

◤ Tony Harris in hospital in 2009

⬇ Help for Heroes assists in the delivery of world-class prosthetics and recovery for injured service personnel

⬊ Band of Brothers member on climbing activity with Battle Back

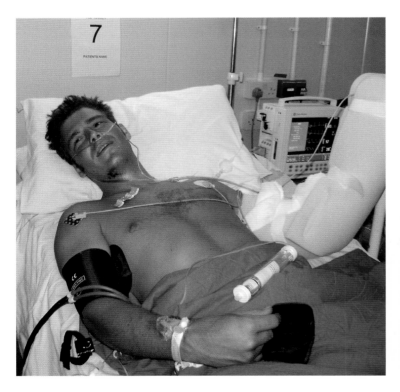

TEDWORTH HOUSE

Tedworth House is one of four Recovery Centres run by Help for Heroes, which forms part of the Defence Recovery Capability. Tedworth House aims to inspire the wounded, injured and sick and returning veterans to lead active, independent and fulfilling lives, which will enable them to reach their full potential and to support them and their families for life. It is a place of opportunities providing education, training, sport and adventure in a relaxed, understanding and caring environment. State of the art facilities and dedicated staff aid the road to recovery.

Tedworth House includes the Phoenix Centre gym which has some of the UK's most advanced sporting facilities, including a Skiplex, SwimEx, strength and conditioning room with adaptive equipment, steam room, sauna, and sports hall with a sprung floor. There are 54 bedrooms (including four family suites), multiple classrooms and IT facilities, an art and games room as well as quieter spaces for leisure and relaxation.

As a 'one-stop welfare shop' the Support Hub at Tedworth House brings together a range of service charities, agencies and organisations to offer advice, guidance and support on a multitude of issues such as money, health, housing, employment and respite. The Support Hub is available to serving and veteran wounded, injured and sick personnel from all three services, along with their families and carers.

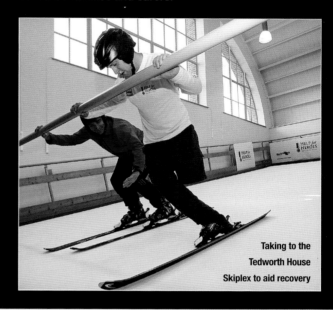

Taking to the Tedworth House Skiplex to aid recovery

RACE2RECOVERY
AIMS

Race2Recovery is a team primarily of injured and disabled British and US servicemen comprising drivers, navigators and support crew. They are all volunteers with the shared aim of inspiring those who are injured, disabled or facing adversity at the same time as raising much-needed funds for the service charities that have helped them on their way since injury.

The objective of the Race2Recovery team was to enter and then complete the famous 5,500-mile Dakar Rally in 2013. Powered by Land Rover Defender-based Wildcat vehicles, they would race in the blistering South American sun for as much as 400 miles a day at speeds of up to 100mph. It would take two gruelling

← US Marine Mark Zambon uses shorter prosthetics to give him more room in the confines of the rally car

⬇ Some of the Race2Recovery Dakar team at scrutineering in Lima

weeks to cross some of the harshest terrain on the planet, in parts of Peru, Argentina and Chile.

Two daunting statistics at the back of their minds would be the fact that fewer than half of the competing vehicles reach the finish line and that over 50 lives have been claimed since the rally's inception in 1978. It's hard enough for an able-bodied team to complete the Dakar, but it would really test the physical capabilities, strength and resolve of these brave men. If they succeeded, they would make history as the first team of disabled drivers ever to complete the Dakar.

In parallel with their ambitious target the team have been raising, and continue to raise, money for charitable causes chosen by the injured members of the team. In the UK the money goes to Tedworth House, the Recovery Centre run by Help for Heroes (as part of the Defence Recovery Capability) where injured servicemen can receive every kind of support, forever. In the US the beneficiary is The Heroes Project, which works with injured veterans and soldier families to improve the care and protection of these heroes.

All the charitable money that is donated to Race2Recovery by the public or organisations goes to support Tedworth House and is completely separate from the team's racing activity, which is paid for by personal contribution and corporate sponsorship alone.

In just one year Race2Recovery created a capable and competitive rally team from nothing. The team are spread across the UK (and around the world) and everyone involved in running the team does so in their spare time. All personnel are either in full-time work or servicemen in rehabilitation from injury.

Those members of team who have been wounded in combat have a huge variety of injuries, some more apparent than others, but each person has had their life completely changed. Be it missing limbs, or spinal, respiratory, fragmentation or psychological injuries, each has resolved to prove that their injury will not stop them completing the toughest race on the planet.

⬆ **Mechanics Rick Nixon, Dave Reeve, Sean Whatley and Lee Townsend with driver Ben Gott at team HQ – Keith Gott Landrover**

⬇ **Quin Evans and Tony Harris appreciating the Wildcat engineering**

RACE2RECOVERY
HELP FOR HEROES

Help for Heroes supports veterans and serving personnel who have been wounded, injured or become sick as a result of serving their country. The charity provides immediate, direct support to individuals as well as building long-term provision for the future. Additionally, families and dependants receive support from the charity, as they care for their loved one and help them adapt to the new challenges they will face.

To date, Help for Heroes has spent or allocated £50 million for individual support, including direct grants to over 2,500 individuals through the Quick Reaction Fund, which is administered by the services' own charities. Help for Heroes have also supported many other initiatives with funding, including the Race2Recovery project.

← A hero's welcome

→ Staff Sgt Mark Zambon on his first adventure conquering Kilimanjaro, just 18 months after losing his legs in an IED blast

⬇ Help for Heroes Band of Brothers using the track at the Olympic stadium before it opened – the very first runners on the track

The Heroes Project

This US charity was formed in 2009 by Tim Wayne Medvetz and benefits from funds raised by the US members of the Race2Recovery team. The Heroes Project is a foundation dedicated to raising funds primarily to help wounded warriors climb the world's highest peaks and find renewed purpose in their lives. The foundation's premise is that it can make a difference and change the lives of wounded veterans, soldiers and their families – one soldier, one veteran, one family at a time through three core initiatives:

The Heroes Project supports climbing programmes for wounded soldiers and veterans. After a serious accident left Tim injured and in long-term physical therapy, he vowed he would climb to the summit of Everest, which he ultimately did in 2007. The comeback Tim experienced in conquering that challenge transformed his life. It also inspired him to share the challenge and triumph with those who need it most – wounded warriors – which he has done ever since in a volunteer capacity.

ENDEAVOUR FUND

Towards the end of 2012, only days after they had finished their sand training, the team received the fantastic news that they had been awarded the first ever grant from the Endeavour Fund, which was set up by the Royal Foundation of the Duke and Duchess of Cambridge and Prince Harry to enable more wounded and injured servicemen and women to take part in expeditions and sporting challenges as part of their recovery.

At the launch of the Fund, earlier in 2012, Prince Harry said: 'I am delighted that our Foundation is launching the Endeavour Fund. We must never forget the terrible price so many of our men and women in uniform have paid – and continue to pay – to keep us free and safe.'

The team, needless to say, were thrilled, as Tony Harris explained: 'This financial backing from the Endeavour Fund will enable us to realise our dreams of becoming the first disability team to compete in the Dakar. Not only that, but the Foundation has recognised that our campaign goes further than just racing and that we're aiming to inspire other people who may be injured, sick or facing adversity. We now hope we can increase awareness of Race2Recovery and, in turn, increase our fundraising activity.'

RACE2RECOVERY
THE CHALLENGE

Both a motor race and an orienteering challenge, the Dakar Rally pits some of the world's finest long-distance rally drivers against amateur competitors. For the latter, the event is often the culmination of their dreams, and they come eager to take up the challenge with their motorcycles, cars, quad bikes and trucks. The Dakar attracts competitors of more than 50 nationalities who are watched on television by over a billion viewers in 190 countries.

Far more than just a simple question of racing skill and speed, the Dakar requires off-road navigational skills and consistency. In this form of long-distance rally discipline, endurance prevails and the slightest mistake costs dearly. This combination of physical toughness and technical performance has attracted champions from many different backgrounds, all keen to measure themselves against each other while tackling this unique event.

⬇ **Belgian Pascal Feryn tackles the sand seas in his Toyota Landcruiser**

There's no escaping the fact that the Dakar is an expensive undertaking and Race2Recovery wouldn't have been able to enter but for considerable technical and logistical support from Land Rover and generous sponsorship from a wide range of companies. In the early days, the Race2Recovery campaign comprised just one Land Rover Freelander and a handful of members, but Land Rover became the first major sponsor and paved the way for other companies to step in too.

'The way the team developed in 18 months is phenomenal – from a few guys with a Land Rover and a seemingly unrealistic dream of competing in the Dakar, to a team of 28 with a fleet of race and support vehicles,' said Andrew 'Pav' Taylor, the team's manager.

There were heartbreaking and stressful periods, however, when it looked like all the hard work had been in vain because the money was close to running out. But thanks to dogged determination and – crucially – a grant in November 2012 from The Royal Foundation's Endeavour Fund, the way was finally clear for the team to realise its goal.

DAKAR BACKGROUND

It all began in 1977 when Thierry Sabine got lost on his motorcycle in the Libyan desert during the Abidjan–Nice Rally. Saved from the sands, he returned to his native France still inspired by the landscape and dreamed up a rally that would start in Paris and finish in Dakar, Senegal. He coined a motto for his inspiration: 'A challenge for those who go. A dream for those who stay behind.'

The first Paris–Dakar Rally, which started in December 1978, attracted 170 competitors and was a challenge true to Sabine's vision, with a 10,000km route to Senegal through Algeria, Niger, Mali and Upper Volta. Motorcyclist Cyril Neveu, on a Yamaha 500 XT, was the first of 74 trailblazers to make it to the finish in Dakar.

Since then this unique event has generated innumerable sporting and human stories. Stéphane Peterhansel has become the most successful competitor, with an incredible record: he made his début in 1988 in the motorcycle category for Yamaha and went on to win six times between 1991 and 1998; then he switched to cars and achieved another five victories, with Mitsubishi in 2004, 2005 and 2007, and with Minis in 2012 and 2013.

The rally was cancelled in 2008 due to terrorist activities in Mauretania and thereafter it transferred from Africa to South America, retaining the name 'Dakar' because that one word so powerfully evokes the ultimate rallying challenge.

'Taking on the Dakar shows everyone what injured people can do and that life doesn't stop. It's not just the driving, there's so much behind the scenes — fundraising, fixing the vehicles and working as a team...'

Captain Tony Harris

RACE2RECOVERY
THE TEAM

The Race2Recovery team is manned by volunteers and drawn predominantly from wounded service personnel, veterans and expert civilians to create a team capable of competing in international rally raids with the ultimate goal of completing the Dakar Rally. There was never a need to 'recruit' personnel: after the fledgling team's appearance on BBC TV's *Top Gear* in August 2011 with their modest Land Rover Freelander, there were regular offers of help. The tom-toms within the rallying fraternity and military circles also spread the word and brought many offers of assistance and volunteers, some of whom were able to make it on to the full racing team.

⬆ Tony Harris describes dunes with retired US Marine Corps Colonel Mike Kurth from Boeing UK

One of the main problems with running a team of volunteers from so many areas of life, including military personnel tied by operational requirements, was that not all team members could meet at all locations for training or rally events.

Despite this there was a logistical need for a permanent base and the team set up headquarters in Hampshire at Keith Gott Landrover, where civilian team member Ben is a partner in the family business. Thankfully there was enough space to accommodate the growing collection of vehicles and to provide rudimentary billets for team members and the working parties who slept over at weekends when possible in order to ensure that all necessary work got done.

Work on the vehicles and equipment had to fit round daily routines, as anyone with volunteering experience knows, with weekends, days off and round-the-clock all-nighters required to make the deadline – in achieving the Dakar dream every member of the team had a vital role to play.

Over the following pages let's meet everyone in the team, from drivers and navigators to mechanics and instructors.

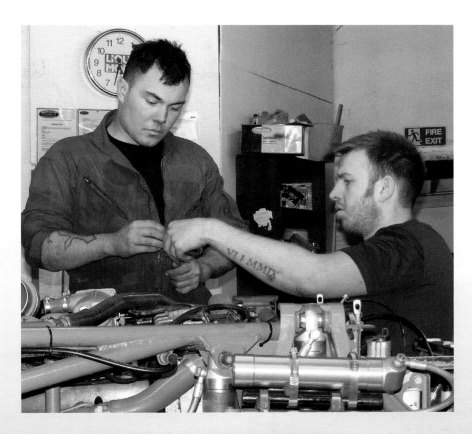

⬆ Tim Read and 'Baz' Whittingham compare tattoos over a Wildcat engine. Below: The team on arrival at the bivouac in Lima, Peru ready for their Dakar challenge

Team Manager (and Race2Recovery co-founder)
Warrant Officer Class 1 Andrew 'Pav' Taylor
Royal Army Medical Corps

It's one of life's mysteries why Andrew is known as 'Pav', but the name suits him. An Army veteran of 24 years, Pav began his military career in the first Gulf War when he joined the Royal Army Medical Corps at the age of 18. He can boast an extensive tour history, having served in Afghanistan and Bosnia four times, Iraq once and Kosovo twice. As well as serving his country, Pav has sailed the Atlantic, trekked in the Himalayas, is an avid Manchester United fan and a dedicated family man.

'I have a very supportive and loving wife,' he says. 'We got married when I was just 20 and had the kids when we were still young. Throughout our marriage, I've been away a lot and often in dangerous places where communication has been difficult, but she's always stood by me and I love her every day for that.'

Pav suffered a serious back injury and a perforated eardrum in 2008 when a suicide bomber drove into his Land Rover. Miraculously, everyone aboard survived, so his injuries might seem a small sacrifice considering what could have happened. However, they still plague him to this day and he's had to undergo a number of operations, including spinal fusion of his lower back, which left him bedridden for 12 weeks. Pav is now medically discharged from the Army and is adjusting to life on 'Civvy Street'. He is a co-founder and Team Manager of Race2Recovery.

Team Principal Advisor/Navigator Trainer
Quin Evans

Quin met Tony Harris through one of the other drivers, Ben Gott, and jumped straight into the car with Tony to enter the Borders Hill Rally. He was signed up to the team there and then, after suitably impressing the guys with his gentle nature yet confident outlook on life and enthusiasm for the project. Quin has been racing since he was 16 and has taken part in international events for 11 years. He came third in the British Hill Rally Championships in 1997 and finished his first Dakar in 2004.

Unfortunately, Quin had to leave the racing side of the team because of family commitments, and he was replaced as Tony's navigator by Cathy Derousseaux. However, he did remain with the team, providing huge support to the navigators as he led and wrote programmes for them, to make sure they were fully prepared and ready for the big event, and then in December 2012 he replaced Pierre de Frenne as Team Principal Advisor due to Pierre's ill health.

Injured personnel are naturally the focus of the Race2Recovery endeavour of triumph over adversity and their biographies make compelling reading. Supporting them all the way are their able-bodied team companions with all the necessary expertise to take on the Dakar Rally, from mechanics to off-road driving experts. Meet this truly remarkable team.

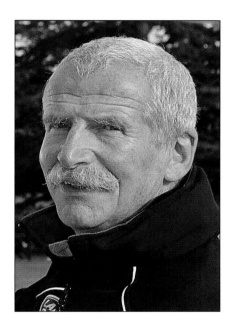

Team Principal Advisor
Pierre de Frenne

The team were thrilled to have on board the expertise and skill of Belgian motorsport entrepreneur Pierre de Frenne. Pierre founded his company, Donerre, in 1994, and it's based in the South of France. Specialising in suspension fittings and dampers, Donerre has experience of over 25 million racing miles. Pierre knows a lot of people in the racing world and was keen to become involved as soon as he heard about the Race2Recovery mission. His expertise became invaluable, and to have the quality of Donerre parts on the cars made the idea of reaching the finish of the Dakar seem much more plausible.

'I fly to and from France regularly and with the internet it has been easy,' he said. 'I give the guys advice and am thrilled to have our suspension parts on the vehicles. My company has been very successful over the last 18 years, winning numerous awards. When I started it up, I wanted to show people that suspension has a human element. Today, there are over 50,000 rally cars with Donerre suspension and I'm proud of that figure. We have a good reputation and many of the cars fitted with our parts have won Dakar Rallies.'

Pierre's military background is limited, although when he was 20 he did do a year's national service in Belgium, which means he understands some of the humour and jokes bandied around by the other team members. Sadly, in December 2012 he suffered serious medical complications and was unable to carry on with his role or travel to South America with the team. Quin Evans, one half of the original racing pairs who had to leave due to family commitments, replaced him as Team Principal Advisor.

Meet the eight people – seven men and one woman – charged with driving and navigating the four-car Race2Recovery team in the T1 Class (for petrol-engined 4x4 improved cross-country vehicles weighing less than 3,500kg). The aim of each driver/navigator pair was to get their Wildcat vehicle across the finish line. It was a demanding 'ask', but then they were part of a uniquely determined team.

*'I used to worry
about packing enough
socks, now I have to think
about packing enough legs.'*
Captain Tony Harris

Driver (and Race2Recovery co-founder)
Captain Anthony (Tony) Harris
2nd Battalion, Royal Regiment of Fusiliers

Having served two years in Northern Ireland and done three tours of Iraq, Tony Harris was seriously injured in 2009 while serving with the Royal Regiment of Fusiliers in Sangin, Afghanistan. His Jackal patrol vehicle was blown up by an IED (improvised explosive device) and the blast shattered both of his ankles and his left elbow. After ten months of slow recuperation and dealing with a marauding infection, he made the decision to have one of his legs amputated below the knee. It was a brave choice, but Tony has adjusted well to life with a prosthetic limb. He knows, though, that he couldn't have done it without support from his wife, Liz, and their two young children, Felix and Emily.

'Taking on the Dakar shows everyone what injured people can do and that life doesn't stop. It's not just the driving, there's so much behind the scenes – fundraising, fixing the vehicles and working as a team, even when you haven't slept for three days and the heat is unbearable,' said Tony. 'I've never been a person who's obsessed with exhausts or gearboxes, but I have learnt so much thanks to Race2Recovery. Although I think cars and machinery are real dark magic, I love being the Sorcerer's Apprentice!'

Something one can't fail to notice about Tony is his grin and 'cheeky chappy' humour. Packing for a training exercise one weekend, his dry wit shone through when he Tweeted: 'I used to worry about packing enough socks, now I have to think about packing enough legs.'

Navigator/co-driver
Cathy Derousseaux

This lady doesn't need any sympathy for being the only female on the racing team – she can definitely hold her own. Cathy comes from incredible racing stock and has been co-driving since she was 16. Her godfather, Pierre Lartigue, three-times Dakar champion and a four-times world rallye raid champion, is close friends with Pierre de Frenne (Team Principal Advisor). But that connection was just one reason why Cathy's name was put forward in October 2012 as replacement navigator for Quin Evans (see page 22).

Still only 24, Cathy is a professional driver and a student, studying for a Master of Management of Sport. She's the only elite motorsport woman competing in France and also the only woman to have co-driven in the Middle East; she has won the Lebanese Championships as well as the French Championships three times in a row.

'Being involved with R2R tugs at my heartstrings as my grandmother was an amputee, due to diabetes – although she lived until she was 90! I also didn't have to think twice before I said yes, as I've done the Dakar before, in 2007, and there's no other race like it on the planet. And to do it in the knowledge that you're with men and women who are now injured as a result of such selfless acts, how could anyone say no?'

Driver
Ben Gott

Off-road rallying, cars and anything with wheels have been in Ben Gott's blood for as long as he can remember. With no military background, but with the utmost respect for what the guys have sacrificed during their time serving Queen and country, Ben would be at the helm of one of the Wildcats with US Marine Mark Zambon as his co-driver.

Ben is a partner in the family's Land Rover business and Go Raid, an Off-Road logistics company that caters for events such as the Dakar Rally. In 2010 he took time off to concentrate on building his Dakar-spec Qt Wildcat and, just one year later, completed the rally in his T5 truck, acting as a service vehicle for Giniel de Villiers, who finished third overall.

Navigator
Staff Sergeant Mark Zambon
United States Marine Corps

Mark Zambon, who joined the team in the latter part of 2012, is one of two Americans involved in Race2Recovery and is an injured serviceman. At the age of 27, he has sacrificed more than most to be where he is today. Mark completed deployments in Iraq in 2007 and was also part of Operation Enduring Freedom in 2008 and 2010. In May 2010 he sustained traumatic amputations to three distal joints of his left hand, but his desire to return to full duty did not waver and within six weeks he was back with his men. The team he trained and led executed expert EOD (explosive ordnance disposal) support and disposed of over 50 IEDs, saving marines' lives and limbs.

They say lightning does not strike twice, but in January 2011 Mark was operating in a heavily IED-laden urban area in Sangin, Afghanistan, when he was struck by an IED with a ten-pound explosive main charge. Despite needing serious surgery and prosthetic legs, in August 2011 he embarked on a gruelling training schedule as part of The Heroes Project, with the aim of reaching the summit of Kilimanjaro. After months of pain and honing his climbing prosthetics, he successfully conquered the mountain in July 2012.

'There is a strong and unmistakable message to those who witness individuals triumphing over extreme adversity,' he says. 'I got a big taste of it on the mountain and see the same thing, but on a larger scale, with the Race2Recovery team. As we embrace and triumph over battle injury, watch the team as we all work together as one to finish the most arduous and gruelling race in motorsport.'

'There is a strong and unmistakable message to those who witness individuals triumphing over extreme adversity... As we embrace and triumph over battle injury, watch the team as we all work together as one to finish the most arduous and gruelling race in motorsport.'

Staff Sergeant Mark Zambon (US Marine Corps)

'I do find mixing with the public a struggle at times as I'm very aware that I only have one real limb...Children say what they see and don't have any inhibitions... One seven-year-old kid asked me how I did up my shoelaces, and that made me smile.'

Corporal Tom Neathway

CAR THREE · 440
ORANGE PLANT

Driver
Justin Birchall

Justin only joined the Race2Recovery family late in 2012, replacing Dave Marsh (who left for personal reasons), but his northern humour and over 20 years' experience on the motorsport circuit meant he soon found his place in the team. His family moved to the countryside when Justin was 11, and after that he was never out of his clapped-out Mini, driving round the fields. A few years later, he decided to try out the bike circuit.

'At that time of my life, I was as fit as a flea. Ragging around and controlling a 90kg bike was lots of fun, and I didn't realise just how good it was for keeping fit.' However, as time went on, Justin realised his body didn't bounce as much as it had done and couldn't face the pain of another fracture to his back or a broken leg. Cars seemed a safer choice and, thanks to a family link to Land Rover, he hasn't looked back and has taken part in the British Cross-Country Championships for the past eight years. Justin admits that when he first saw the Race2Recovery team on training exercises in 2011, he looked at them and wondered what they were doing.

'Motorsport is a very cliquey sport, and when these new guys turned up on the circuit everyone thought they wouldn't last. I'm so pleased we were proved wrong. After seeing them at a third meet in Wales I went over and had a chat with them – and the rest, as they say, is history. About a year later, I got a call from Tom asking me if I wanted to drive in the Dakar. After a millisecond of thinking about it and, of course, checking with my wife, I screamed "Yes" and before I knew it my training schedule and nutrition pack were sitting on the doormat.'

Navigator
Corporal Tom Neathway
2nd Battalion, Parachute Regiment

At the age of just 28, Tom Neathway will be spending the rest of his life with three prosthetic limbs. After signing up to the Parachute Regiment 11 years ago, Tom is a veteran of multiple tours of Northern Ireland, Iraq and Afghanistan. On his last tour of Afghanistan, in 2008, Tom triggered a booby trap while covering his platoon moving forward. The blast took off both his feet, while an infection soon afterwards sadly led to the amputation of both his legs and his left arm.

'Much of my recovery and recuperation were done at Headley Court, which is where I met Tony Harris. We shared a room and formed a great bond. I didn't realise Tony was an officer until we'd had a few beers in the bar. I do find mixing with the public a struggle at times as I'm very aware that I only have one real limb. No-one's ever been horrible to me; it's in my head. One guy even came up to me in a petrol station and shook my hand. Children say what they see and don't have any inhibitions, which is why I'm looking at a teaching career when all this is over. One seven-year-old kid asked me how I did up my shoelaces, and that made me smile.'

Driver (and Race2Recovery co-founder)
Major Matt O'Hare
Royal Regiment of Fusiliers

Matt O'Hare served alongside Tony Harris in the Royal Regiment of Fusiliers and has completed multiple tours, including Afghanistan, where he was Mentioned in Dispatches for courage and leadership.

As well as being one of the charity's co-founders, he also leads the team's fundraising efforts. Tony and Matt are great friends; they've been each other's best men and Matt is also godfather to Tony's daughter, Emily. It's not surprising that their bond is so extraordinary as it could quite easily have been Matt, instead of Tony, who ended up with life-changing injuries that fateful day. They're now closer than ever and are the masterminds behind Race2Recovery. On a lighter note, the 'in' joke within the team is that Matt sometimes feels left out because he's one of its very few non-injured members. In the build-up to the Dakar he decided to shatter one of his elbows, and he also broke his pelvis just before his wedding day. His wife Camilla has since tried to hide his motorbike, but all her efforts seem to be in vain as his injuries have not made him see sense...

'It's a massive anti-climax coming back from a tour, but it's nothing like living with lifelong injuries. The outlook on life is a bit greyer, but the Dakar is a huge motivation for all the guys, not just for the injured members. It will be such an achievement if we cross the line – and the memories will last forever. The camaraderie and teamwork we've had will be hugely missed by all of us and this event will replace that, albeit for a relatively short time. It will be sad when it's over, and I know we'll miss the closeness and the relationships we've formed over the last 18 months, but that's no reason not to take up the challenge.'

Navigator/mechanic
Corporal Phillip ('Barney') Gillespie
Royal Irish Regiment

Poor 'Barney', as he's called, seems to be the brunt of many of the team's jokes, but he gives as good as he gets and has no problem laughing at himself. Although he's the baby of the team, at 22, he's already a veteran of Afghanistan. A corporal from the Royal Irish Regiment, Barney was part way through his third tour when he stood on an IED during a routine foot patrol. He suffered multiple injuries to his right leg and lost it below the knee but, unbelievably, he was out of hospital within a month. After six operations – and only five months after sustaining his injuries – his unshakable determination saw him join Race2Recovery as a member of the mechanical team.

'I couldn't have done it without my girlfriend, Kirsty. She was with me at every stage, even during the bad times when I'm sure I was a complete nightmare. There's no doubt that it's incredibly difficult to adjust to having a prosthetic limb, but there's still a life to live and this message is what we hope to get across to everyone out there.'

'It's a massive anti-climax coming back from a tour, but nothing like living with lifelong injuries... but the Dakar is a huge motivation for all the guys, not just for the injured members.'

Major Matt O'Hare

The T4 vehicle is a big, powerful unit with three men on board and its main purpose on the Dakar Rally is to act as a support vehicle to the T1 competitors on special stages. The T4 Truck class, also known as *Camions* (Lorries), is made up of vehicles weighing more than 3,500kg that compete in their own T4 classification. Alongside them are the T5 vehicles, rally support trucks that move from bivuoac to bivouac to support the racing vehicles.

'I was initially approached to fit a roll cage and then, on meeting the team, found an inspiring group of people whom I wanted to support.'

Chris Ratter

T4 Driver and Driver Trainer
Mark Cullum

Mark Cullum is an Operational Watch Commander in the Hereford & Worcester Fire & Rescue Service and specialises in water rescue and off-road driver training. He was formerly an army reservist and has served all over the globe. Mark has been deeply involved with Race2Recovery since appearance on BBC TV's *Top Gear* in 2011.

Having finished second in the Camel Trophy, Mark is the ideal man to drive the T4 truck and is also well-placed to instruct the team on all matters concerning driving. He led the team's driver training exercise in Morocco – and all the team's drivers now fear his 'Traction, Ground Clearance and Stability' chat! He has also assisted Land Rover with global vehicle events and new model launches.

Finance and Business Advisor/T4 Co-Driver
Charles Sincock
Ex-Irish Guards

Charles Sincock has a head for numbers and is invaluable to the team in offering financial guidance and business advice. In March 2011 he met Tony in a pub, and Tony proceeded to explain the inspiration behind

Race2Recovery and ask if Charles would give the team financial guidance. Although already a busy man, working in London in Private Equity, Charles couldn't say 'no'. And he didn't want to either, because the draw of being involved once again with the 'lads' and their army banter was too strong. Charles was in the Irish Guards for six years working with British and US Forces in the second Gulf War. From the moment he heard about Race2Recovery Charles saw the benefits, and he now plays a very active role. Many of the patrons who have come on board are involved thanks to his persuasive tongue, and this vital aspect of the charity has operated healthily under his guidance.

T4 Navigator
Chris Ratter

Chris Ratter runs a business specialising in motorsport engineering on cross-country vehicles and support trucks. He has also competed, with some success, in various national and international events as a driver and a co-driver. With oil under his fingertips and a sense of calm whatever the situation, Chris's role is to support the team with all aspects of vehicle preparation – including, of course, making sure the T4 and the T5 DAF support truck are ready to go.

'I was initially approached to fit a roll cage and then, on meeting the team, found an inspiring group of people whom I wanted to support. Not only do I have new friends but I can also now say that I'm going to the 2013 Dakar Rally – and that's amazing!'

Technical Stores Manager
Corporal Gareth Paterson
Royal Electrical and Mechanical Engineers (REME)

'I'm one of the longest-serving military men on the team and joined back in 1994,' says Gareth Paterson. 'I wanted to give something back to the charities that have helped me and found Race2Recovery was the perfect way to do it. I'm massively excited about everything and feel like a kid in a sweetshop!'

Gareth is married to Nikki, who was paralysed after a motorbike accident. She still gives him more than a run for his money when it comes to all things competitive, however, as she is a potential Paralympian for the next Winter Games – her sport of choice is the skeletal luge, although she also enjoys rock climbing and sky diving.

As Technical Stores Manager, Gareth has a big and important job to do: every piece of equipment, lubricant or tool has to be accounted for, and if anything is broken or needs replacing he's the man who puts in the orders and makes sure there are enough tools available.

Mobility Training and Driver Support
Warrant Officer Marty Rae
9 Parachute Squadron Royal Engineers

Marty Rae is the oldest-serving injured squaddie in the team, having joined up in 1985 and due to be medically discharged in April 2013. In September 2007 he was engaged in fire at close quarters in Iraq after entering a burning building and was extremely lucky to get out alive and to survive the 30 rounds that poured down on him.

'I never saw the guy and I couldn't believe I made it out alive. As a result, I lost my right forearm due to gunshot wounds in my elbow. I was also shot through my night-vision goggles and had shrapnel in my left wrist. I could feel the bullets in my right arm straight away, as my weapon just fell to the floor, and I knew I was in a bad situation. I've had over a dozen operations in the last five years, including skin grafts and nerve grafts taken from my legs, but I think I'm done now.'

A friend of Mark Cullum, Marty's involvement with Race2Recovery began when he discovered that a role needed to be filled in the team and so he offered his services without hesitation – his task has been to work closely with Mark Cullum on the mobility training programme. On the Dakar itself Marty is also the driver for the Team Principal Advisor and Team Manager.

'I wanted to give something back to the charities that have helped me and found Race2Recovery was the perfect way to do it. I'm massively excited about everything and feel like a kid in a sweetshop!'

Corporal Gareth Paterson

T5 Driver
Corporal Daniel 'Baz' Whittingham
11 EOD Regiment (Explosive Ordnance Disposal), Royal Logistics Corps

'Baz' Whittingham, who was injured in Afghanistan during a route clearance in Sangin, is part of the support team as a driver of one of the T5 vehicles. As part of the IEDD (Improvised Explosive Device Disposal) team, he drove his vehicle over an IED and of the two occupants he came off the worst by far. After being thrown out of the vehicle, he woke up to the news that he had broken his pelvis, part of his back, both his legs and was also suffering from a collapsed lung. He spent three days in intensive care, three months in hospital and six months in a wheelchair, before being able to walk again ten months later.

He met Tony Harris and 'Barney' Gillespie at Headley Court during his recovery, and also knew Gareth Paterson, who had been an instructor while Baz was completing his basic training. Baz had heard about the R2R endeavour and admits to being a bit of pest. 'I sent Tony loads of emails, begging to be involved in whatever capacity.'

Baz is waiting to be discharged from the army and is determined to keep busy and get back to real life after the Dakar. Six weeks after being blown up he agreed to row the Atlantic as a member of Row2Recovery (but had to pull out just before the start for medical reasons), and he has also taken part in an Iron Man challenge and swum round Jersey.

Mechanic and T5 Support Truck Driver
Martyn Williams
45 Commando Royal Marines

The baby of the support team, at 23, is Martyn Williams. He does get a bit of stick from the other guys for being in the Marines, but he just shrugs and says you can't beat the Green Beret. He joined back in 2006 but was injured in 2008 when he was blown up by an IED. His left foot was his only serious injury, and after much rest and recuperation he is now fully fit and still in active service. In July 2012 Martyn was the lucky person chosen to deliver the Olympic Flame to London, flying in by Royal Navy Sea King helicopter before an abseil into the Tower of London. Martyn is set to go back to serve in Afghanistan in April 2013.

'I'm the only one on the team who was injured but is now fit again, so I know I'm a lucky guy,' he says. 'Although I'm the "baby" I think I'm more mature, at times, than some of the older guys on the team!'

Race2Recovery would be nowhere without these guys. Their work behind the scenes is phenomenal and their expertise is staggering. Without the insight and advice of the mechanics and the efforts of all those involved in fundraising, PR and corporate work over the past two years, not to mention social media and patrons, the team's achievements would have been just a dream.

Technical Support
Sean Whatley
Ex-Royal Electrical and Mechanical Engineers (REME)

Gareth Paterson is partnered on the support team by ex-REME colleague Sean Whatley, who served in Iraq and Bosnia during the 1990s.

During his time in the Army, Sean was a mechanic for a hill rally team and he was also a member of the first British Army team to compete in Rhino Charge 1996 in Kenya. His role on the Dakar Rally is lead mechanic on one of the Wildcats.

Logistics Support Co-ordinator (LSC)
John Winskill
Ex-Royal Scots Regiment

Although he works for a very high-profile company, Boeing, with a title to match, John Winskill is a self-confessed 'nutter' who loves doing things that are a little crazy. That's the reason why the Race2Recovery endeavour first caught his eye, back in May 2012. An email to social media guru Debbie Harrison (Dave Reeve's wife) was all it took for John to become part of R2R. After a meeting with Tony in London, he was soon organising training days and sorting out satellite communications as well as adopting the nickname 'travelbooking.co – thanks to his adeptness at booking flights at the last minute! A man with the facts at his fingertips, he knows all the intricate details surrounding the Dakar Rally and can't do enough to support the guys.

Before Boeing and R2R, John was a military man who spent 13 years in the Royal Scots Regiment, hanging up his beret in 2006. He suffered a shoulder injury during his service but is now fully recovered.

'I've a built a Land Rover from scratch and would describe myself as a true enthusiast, but I'm completely uncoordinated. I was all ready to go to the Dakar Rally in 2008 but it was cancelled – I couldn't believe it! I've been obsessed with the race since I was a boy so now, at the age of 42, this is definitely my time to experience it right from the front line – and I'm doing it for an incredible cause too.'

Mechanic
Corporal Tim Read
US Marine Corps

One of the youngest of R2R's amputees, 23-year-old Tim joined the team late in 2012, at the same time as fellow American Mark Zambon. Tim understands only too well the drive and desire to succeed after suffering a serious injury in a shooting incident in Helmand province in October 2010. His injury, however, hasn't changed his attitude to combat and defending his country, despite personal sacrifice.

'All I remember is my ears ringing, feeling debris hit my face and closing my eyes. When I opened them I looked at my hands and they were shattered. I still had both boots on but was in absolutely indescribable pain. I lost my left leg, but nothing else – and when I say nothing else, I mean that as I am the exact same Marine that loves his life, his country and the corps.'

Mechanic
Staff Sergeant Chris Astles
Royal Electrical and Mechanical Engineers (REME)

Chris Astles is a Staff Sergeant from the REME and is a superb vehicle mechanic having passed the notoriously complex Artificers course. This means he's the perfect person to support the team as a T5 driver and be on hand to support the mechanics as and when required.

Mechanic
Lee Townsend
Royal Artillery

Lee Townsend is a man who has served his country and suffered for it. He joined the Royal Electrical and Mechanical Engineers (REME) in 1989 as a mechanic and spent over four years with the Tank Transporters. He served operationally in the first Gulf War and also in Bosnia. Lee's injury to his knees was sustained after a road traffic accident while serving and it took him four months to recover at Headley Court. He then joined the Royal Artillery.

Lee offered his services to the team after hearing about them on the radio. His knowledge and expertise are much valued.

Men and women from all sorts of backgrounds make up the support team. Some have served in the military and, as result, have lost limbs themselves or now live with other permanent injuries; others are civilians who just love anything to do with cars and have a wealth of knowledge at their fingertips.

T1 Chief Mechanic
Dave Reeve

Dave Reeve can usually be found quietly getting on with the job, with his head under a bonnet – being around a lot of rowdy servicemen can take its toll! Amazingly, Dave had never been on an aircraft until he he travelled with R2R to South America.

Mechanic
Tim Hare

Tim Hare has been in motorsport for over 22 years with over a decade in Formula One. His current role with Bosch motorsport gave him the opportunity to supplement hardware support by providing technical expertise to the team during the Dakar.

Mechanic
Chris Bayliss

Chris makes up one half of the Bayliss team, who run the Land Rover specialists Old Forge Garage in Leadenham, near Lincoln. Chris brings a degree of old-school engineering (commonly known as the hammer approach) and a phenomenal amount of experience.

Mechanic
Phill Bayliss

Phill Bayliss, son of Chris, is very fortunate that his understanding wife, Kate, encouraged him to fulfil a life-long ambition – despite leaving their two-week-old baby – to 'follow his dream' with the Race2Recovery team on the Dakar Rally.

Mechanic
Jonny Koonja

Jonny Koonja joined the team as a mechanic for the Orange Plant Wildcat. He demonstrated his own racing skill on the Tuareg Rally alongside Race2Recovery driver Justin Birchall, and also co-drives Dan Lofthouse in British Cross Country Championship) events.

Mechanic
Rick Nixon

Rick Nixon has been involved with the Race2Recovery team through the British Cross Country Championship, where he works with Chris Ratter. He has previously built seven cars for the Dakar Rally and was Chief Mechanic for five of the cars on the event in 2006.

RACE2RECOVERY
FRIENDS AND FAMILY

What happens to those people left at home, the 'next of kin' who receive that dreaded phone call or knock at the door? Of course, family members always hope that every time their loved ones go on tour they will come back safely and life will continue as normal, but inevitably they are on edge every single minute of every single day in case the worst happens and their men are flown home for urgent medical attention.

Liz Taylor
Andrew 'Pav' Taylor's wife

If you met Pav (Andrew Taylor), you'd question whether he was injured at all. As his wife Liz explains: 'It can be hard for Pav as his injuries aren't on display; he doesn't have a prosthetic limb so his pain can't be seen. I'm not saying that this means it's worse for him; it's just different. He's on constant pain relief and wears a morphine patch every day. Plus he's older than the other lads so it does take its toll.'

When Pav was injured by a suicide bomber in 2008, Liz received the phone call at work. Unbelievably, she listened to what had happened, put the phone down and continued her working day. Looking back, she understands now how her reactions were a coping mechanism: 'I'm not heartless. I think I just went on autopilot; 2008 was a bad year for the family. My eldest daughter was being very badly bullied at school and then getting the news about Pav was like someone out there was really trying to test my resolve and strength.'

Liz and Pav celebrated their 20th wedding anniversary in 2011 and they're proof that a strong family unit can overcome adversity and even make a couple stronger. 'The Army provided us with a good life and, looking back, I wouldn't change anything,' she says. 'There were times I won't miss – like getting home from work on a Friday evening and finding a post-it note on the fridge from Pav, saying that he'd gone away and wasn't sure when he'd be back. There are still dark days for us both, but we work through them together. He's waiting for a final release date, but I don't know where he would have been without R2R, it really has been a saving grace for him. I can see how much he loves the project, despite working so hard and being constantly glued to his mobile!'

'It can be hard for Pav as his injuries aren't on display; he doesn't have a prosthetic limb so his pain can't be seen.'

Liz Taylor, wife of Andrew 'Pav' Taylor, Team Manager

Julia Molony and Liz Harris
Tony Harris's mother and wife

It was slightly different for Tony's mum, Julia, when she found out that Tony had been blown up, because she wasn't listed as his next of kin. She heard the news from her daughter-in-law, Liz.

'I did get a phone call later from Tony himself, but I couldn't understand a word he said as he was dosed up on morphine and a cocktail of other drugs. I didn't resent not being told first as, although I'm his mother, I have a lovely daughter-in-law and he has his own family who, quite rightly, are his priority. There are many mothers with sons serving who don't have the relationship I have with Liz and only find out days later, which must be just horrendous. I'm very lucky.'

Julia admits to being in complete shock for 18 months, and even when Tony was discharged from hospital she still found it very difficult to comes to terms with what had happened to her son.

'When the decision was made to amputate Tony's leg, I couldn't be there when he came round. I was asked but I needed to digest what had happened to him – it was a real low point for me. I went to see him the day after but just dissolved into tears. I wanted to be strong for him but I didn't behave like I thought I would, the emotions took over completely. I couldn't take his pain away and I couldn't make it better. A kiss wasn't enough, not that time. Tony just looked at me and said, "Mum, I understand, it's your leg really, you made it." I fell apart after he said that.'

Tony has now been medically discharged and is adapting to civilian life with his prosthetic leg – a nine-to-five working day is something to get used to but, as Julia explains, 'I'm incredibly lucky. He's alive and I can see him and call him whenever I want; some parents have had that brutally taken away from them. It's not easy when people say "You must be so grateful he's alive" as yes, I am obviously, but it's not helpful as it stops you from feeling what you want to feel and the guilt is awful.'

Liz had only given birth to their baby girl, Emily, two weeks before Tony was injured and already had two-year-old Felix to look after. As she recalls, 'I remember that it was a Thursday when I got the call. I was told that Tony would be in Birmingham on the Saturday but, like many families do, I didn't want to move up there and disrupt Felix's routine. Of course I was there when he was flown in and by his side as much as I could be. Thank goodness for Julia, she was great looking after the children and also me, when I needed a shoulder to cry on.'

Tony was in and out of hospital for months and suffered many infections but Liz was there with him as much as possible while maintaining a 'normal' way of life for the children. 'Having two little kids, there's no choice; you have to get on with it as life doesn't stop, although at times it feels like it's falling down around your ears. Our life was hectic before Tony was blown up – he'd been on three different tours in three different countries and we'd moved house five times – so his injury was just another test for our family. We're now through it and looking forward to life as civilians.

'Race2Recovery has brought out the best in Tony and in many ways suits him more than being an army officer. He will find it difficult to adjust to life outside, but this project is just fantastic for him.'

Marta Zambon
Mark Zambon's wife

For Mark and his wife, Marta, the story is different. They met seven months after he had sustained his injuries and in the summer of 2011 a whirlwind romance soon followed. The wonders of the internet had put these two in touch thanks to an online dating site. Marta spoke fondly of their first meeting: 'We talked online and on the phone every day. After a few months, I decided I wanted to meet this amazing man so I flew from the Czech Republic to San Diego on Mark's birthday. To cut a long story short, we fell in love, moved in together in January 2012 and married eight months later.'

Marta only knows Mark as he is today so there was no harrowing phone call or agonising vigil for her by the side of a hospital bed. But she has witnessed some dark days: 'Although Mark is the most positive person I know, he can lose himself in a place where even I can't reach him. I always try to be there for him and assure him that everything is okay. Sometimes a smile and a kiss work wonders.'

After the Dakar Rally the couple are moving to Florida, where Mark will be teaching at Elgin Air Force base as he is staying in the Marine Corps. It's clear from speaking to these two that they're hopelessly in love and looking forward to a long future together; this is just a chapter in their lives but one that is tremendously important to both of them.

'There's no doubt that R2R is a great project,' says Marta. 'Injury doesn't have to stop your dreams, in fact, it can make you take stock and realise time is short, so go for it. That's exactly what the team are doing every day of their lives. 'I think there should be more projects like R2R and I know, for Mark, this challenge is very special and the cars will cross that finish line, no matter what.'

Rachael Patterson
Tom Neathway's girlfriend

Tom Neathway, navigator of one of the Wildcats and triple amputee, has found love and fun with girlfriend Rachael Patterson. Rachael, 24, is heavily involved with cars and rally driving.

'I've always been a keen driver, and certainly a motorsport fan,' says Rachael. 'I passed my test two weeks after turning 17.'

With the help of her family, Rachael bought a secondhand Peugeot 106 Rallye S2 and signed herself up for the British Trial & Rally Drivers Association (BTRDA) in the Millers Oils Championship for cars up to 1,400cc. Her first outing – on the Wyedean Forest Rally with co-driver Josh Davison – was tough, taking place in the snow and ice of February 2012 with temperatures down to –5 degrees C and sadly resulted in broken suspension on the final stage, but the pair still managed to complete the course to gain the vital experience that helps deliver future success.

Her partnership with Tom will also see some race outings but these will be on tarmac stages to keep her championship with

Josh Davison separate – and she resolves that the racing duo will move up a class in 2014 adding, 'Tom may well be joining me in the Forest Stages but with his own car and co-driver! We'll then see who's the fastest!'

Tom and Rachael became an item in August 2012. They'd originally met the year before when she was working at a motor show as a promotional girl. Back then, she wasn't really interested in a relationship; she was a racer and was just loving being on the circuit.

'It was great to meet the guys, including Tom, and hear all about R2R. I was in the Army briefly and you can't help but fall in love with the guys in some way or another, despite the way they joke about things which cut close to the bone sometimes!' she laughs. 'Tom and I spoke quite a lot in the year leading up to getting together officially, but it just wasn't the right time for either of us when we first met.'

Rachael doesn't hide the fact that although she met Tom after his injuries and was fully aware of his difficulties, it isn't always plain sailing. 'It's the little things that we both miss being able to do together like dog walking and horse riding – we're both outdoorsy types. Tom can't come with me and he would love to ramble in the countryside, but it's not possible. We're looking at booking a holiday at the moment, and things like access play a huge part in our decision-making.

'Tom does have bad days, like we all do, but the next day it's all forgotten and we move on. He likes to try to do things for himself because he's independent, and quite feisty when he wants to be! After spending time with the guys, and knowing them as I do, the last thing they want is to be mollycoddled. They want to try to do things and if they can't, they will ask. Don't dive in and offer help at once. It's an easy mistake to make but one you probably won't make again.

'Tom is very ambitious and has a whole list of things he wants to do after the Dakar, including stage rallying. He's really got the bug, so in 2013 we are going to try and do a rally together. We did one in 2012 but my clutch failed on the first day so that was the end of that.'

Rachael and Tom have had a few interesting encounters with the general public. 'One afternoon we were in a supermarket and a little girl pointed to Tom and said, "Mummy, there's a robot over there!" We both laughed it off, but there is a lot of metal on his body and she was just saying what she saw. Older people can sometimes be worse as they just stare or, at the other end of the scale, they come up to Tom and shake his hand, especially the old boys from the forces.'

'We were in a supermarket and a little girl pointed to Tom and said, "Mummy, there's a robot over there!" We both laughed it off, but there is a lot of metal on his body and she was just saying what she saw.'

Rachael Patterson, girlfriend of Tom Neathway, Navigator

Camilla O'Hare
Matt O'Hare's wife

Camilla is the wife of the only able-bodied military member of the racing team, Matt. On the tragic day Tony was blown up, it was meant to be Matt, but their duties were swapped at the last minute. The couple only got married in 2011, and due to Dakar training Matt missed their first-year anniversary – he was tackling sand dunes in Morocco at the time. He didn't forget their special day, though, and bought Camilla a fluffy toy and her favourite perfume.

'R2R has taken over lives, but we don't mind,' says Camilla. 'It's such an incredible task to undertake and one of which I am exceedingly proud. Matthew works so hard for the team. Some nights he's on the phone until 1am, conference calls are scheduled slap-bang in the middle of dinner, and our social life has been on hold, really, as weekends haven't existed since March 2012. It's worth all the long hours because it's an amazing and wonderful project.

'I tease Matthew sometimes that he must feel left out, being able-bodied, but since he has been involved with the R2R team he has shattered his elbow and broken his pelvis, thanks to his motorbike. It was very amusing when Tony and Matthew went into a sponsorship meeting together and it was Tony pushing Matt in the wheelchair and he had to introduce Matthew as his able-bodied driver!'

A close family like Camilla's shares her views and also all her fundraising efforts. Her mother and sister help out at all the events they can. Some of her work colleagues have taken part in a sponsored weight-loss programme, and her young nieces have been keen to get involved too.

Kirsty Crawford
Phillip ('Barney') Gillespie's girlfriend

Kirsty Crawford and 'Barney' Gillespie have known each other for years, since they were revising for exams at secondary school. No, they weren't childhood sweethearts, but they were set up by Kirsty's best friend, who passed her phone number to Barney in October 2008 – and they have been together ever since.

Kirsty and Barney were an 'item' before he suffered his injury and it would be silly to state that their lives haven't been changed. But their outlook on what happened to Barney, and as a result their relationship, is very positive and that's one of the reasons they have such a solid partnership.

'I have only seen Barney experience one dark day since his injury and that was very early on when he was still in hospital,' says Kirsty. 'He's exactly the same guy as he was before he lost his leg. I know that sounds unbelievable, but it's true. He's always been a happy-go-lucky kind of person and I know that has really helped his rehab.'

On that dreadful day, it was Barney's father who called Kirsty to tell her the bad news. As they're not married, she isn't the next of kin and therefore she had to wait to learn the details. 'All I wanted to know was that he was alive – that was enough for me. As soon as I knew that he wasn't dead, I knew I could deal with anything. The details were sketchy and we still weren't 100% sure what had happened to him. He was flown to Birmingham and went straight to theatre. He didn't come round until half past ten that night, which meant I had to wait even longer until the next morning to see him. It really did drag on and was one of the longest nights of my life.'

The couple were due to move from their native Northern Ireland to England, but as a result of Barney's injuries they decided to stay put and bought a bungalow. With a few alterations to the layout of the house, such as wider doorways and a shower, Barney leads a completely independent life. He's even hoping to get back into running during 2013.

'He always has something up his sleeve that he wants to conquer next and he won't give up – you may even see him in the London Marathon at this rate!'

Trish Chapman
Widow of Gordon Chapman (Orange Plant)

In a book like this it can be hard not to overdo the superlatives, but Trish Chapman is one lady who deserves all the superlatives in the dictionary. To set the scene, since the very start of Race2Recovery, in 2011, Trish, her daughter Joanna, son Adam and the whole Chapman family have been among the team's strongest supporters, believing in its ability to succeed.

A lover of all things with wheels and large engines, her late husband Gordon commissioned Qt in Plymouth to build his own Wildcat in 2009. Only weeks after it was delivered, he was diagnosed with a terminal brain tumour. It was a dreadful time for all the family. Gordon never got to rally his 'baby' as he passed away in December 2010 and had been too ill in the lead-up to his death to take part in any events.

'After we were introduced to Tom and Tony, we really wanted to support their endeavour financially. The Wildcat was sitting in the garage gathering dust so we loaned it to them on a permanent basis. I didn't want anything back, but I'd inherited Orange Plant and in return the guys branded the car with the logo all over it.

'In 2012 the car was badly damaged at an event, so I realised it was time that the team had full responsibility for it, and its ownership too, so in September 2012 I handed the keys over to Tony. I didn't have to think twice, because I know that I've done exactly what Gordon would have wanted me to do. I'm so thrilled that Gordon's dream is finally being realised.'

The car Trish donated to Race2Recovery is one of the four Wildcats in the team. She has one condition though – that any funds from selling it off, whenever that happens, go straight to Tedworth House.

It's a remarkable gift from a very generous family.

'Gordon loved that car so much and it still makes me wobble to see his name on it. I know he would be so proud knowing that his car was going to the Dakar. What makes it such a pleasure is that they're such good people and so inspiring, both individually as personalities and collectively as a group. They have filled the void in so many ways since I lost Gordon.'

RACE2RECOVERY
THE VEHICLES

'I was approached by Race2Recovery to fit a roll cage and then, on meeting the team, found an inspiring group of people whom I wanted to support...'

Chris Ratter, Renault Kerax (T5) navigator

RACE2RECOVERY
THE VEHICLES

The Race2Recovery team started with one Land Rover Freelander and a handful of people, but by the time the team reached Lima, Peru, for the start of the 2013 Dakar Rally it numbered 28 people and 10 vehicles. The plan was to run four Wildcat racers in the T1 category and alongside them a 4x4 truck that would compete in the T4 class and act as fast support to the Wildcats on the special stages. In addition, the team also had two 8x8 support trucks, acting as mobile workshops and transport for the massive array of spare parts and tools required, as well as two Land Rover Discoveries and one Defender to ferry the team management and mechanics along the 'Assistance' route.

⬇ The Renault Kerax T4 support truck stretches its legs (top); one of the team's support Land Rover Discoveries, 'Slider' (bottom)

FREELANDER

The R2R Freelander is a standard five-door model and is where it all began, with the team making its first appearance in the 2011 British Cross Country Championship before appearing on BBC's *Top Gear*.

Its first outing was in Scotland, on the Borders Hill Rally. This didn't provide the experience that the team was hoping for, though, as flying stones cut the event short. Two rocks knocked the oil filter off the engine and it lost all of its oil. The damage was terminal and the Freelander returned, completely broken, to Dave Reeve's premises in Norfolk. Luckily, a donor vehicle was obtained and the team descended on Norfolk to swap the engine over in a weekend of frantic – and blurred – activity. Fuelled by bacon butties and tea, it was a taste of the incredible teamwork that was to come.

The Freelander has a plumbed-in fire extinguisher system and is a 2.5-litre V6, an automatic model with a standard engine and transmission. It features underbody protection for the engine, gearbox, rear differential, fuel tank and exhaust system, all supplied by Xceed Motorsport.

The vehicle is fitted with a full set of Ohlins modified dampers and the interior has been removed to make way for two race seats with full harnesses. It has been modified with a throttle pedal on the left and right of the brake pedal, so it doesn't matter which side the driver's prosthetic leg is, allowing various members of the team to develop their off-road driving techniques.

RACE2RECOVERY
WILDCAT

SPECIFICATION

Dry weight	1,840kg
Length	3.8m
Height	1.8m
Width	1.8m
Wheelbase	2.69m
Approach angle	70 degrees
Departure angle	68 degrees
Break over	142 degrees
Max gradient	1 in 1
Side slope	40 degrees

RatCat

- Left-hand drive
- Black wing mirrors
- Rover/Buick V8 engine

Joy

- Left-hand drive
- Gold wing mirrors
- Rover/Buick V8 engine

Orange Plant

- Right-hand drive
- Orange wing mirrors
- Jaguar/Land Rover 4-litre V8

When it comes to an event like the Dakar Rally, you need the right tools for the job. And when it comes to vehicles, then the Wildcat definitely fits the bill. A quick look at its pedigree tells the story. It has an enviable reputation at the Dakar, particularly as the car of choice for privateer teams, and has claimed a 12th overall finish.

I.R.D.

- Left-hand drive
- Red wing mirrors
- Jaguar/Land Rover 4-litre V8

Chassis and body

The Wildcat is based on a tubular steel space-frame chassis, creating an extremely rigid safety cell to protect the occupants, while also offering low weight and exceptional strength for the major mechanical component mounting points. The suspension turrets were changed from previous models to accept the Donerre dampers, essential for the harsh conditions the team would face, with hard-packed rocky tracks as well as enormous sand dunes.

The entire frame is cloaked in an easily recognisable, stylish, lightweight composite body shell that is designed to allow panels to be easily replaced as well as removed for servicing and repairs.

The Wildcat uses many parts from the Land Rover range, thanks to their ready availability, strength and reliability.

Storage and fuel

The Wildcat has the capacity to carry 375 litres of fuel, as per FIA regulations, to cope with the incredible distances and rough terrain it will encounter on special stages. The water radiators are mounted at the rear of the vehicle, to keep them protected from the rigours of the desert and potential impacts. The radiators are fed by a roof-mounted air scoop directing air when the vehicle is moving, and twin SPAL electric fans for when the vehicle is stationary.

In addition to carrying fuel, spare oil and other fluids, the Wildcat has space for tools and spare parts so that the crew can carry out minor running repairs, as well as rescue equipment such as sand ladders in case the vehicle gets stuck. Virtually every available space is filled with fluids, parts, tools, water and food, as well as personal safety equipment such as space blankets, in case the occupants are forced to spend a night in the desert, and signalling flares in case of emergency.

Suspension

One of the key areas of improvement during testing was the adoption of the new suspension mountings. These have allowed the Wildcats to be fitted with larger remote-reservoir coil-over Donerre dampers and Suplex springs. The dampers are adjustable in both bump and rebound and this set-up endows the Wildcat with huge suspension travel to cope with rough, high-speed tracks as well as slower, more flowing dunes – and even the huge jumps with heavy landings for which the Dakar is famous.

Engine

Several engine options exist for Wildcats, including petrol V8s and V6 turbo-diesels. However, the team use two petrol versions. Two cars are fitted with the Jaguar/Land Rover 4-litre V8 and two with the slightly older Rover-based petrol V8. Both versions have been modified specifically for the job, and while on paper the power figures appear low – 275bhp and 300lb/ft of torque – it's the way in which the engines deliver their torque that makes the difference.

Both have excellent low-end torque, a characteristic of V8 engines. The Jaguar/Land Rover engine uses variable valve timing to maintain this pulling power – essential for traversing sand and mud as well as climbing dunes – yet allows for improved high-speed performance, essential for the smoother, longer-distance stages. It also offers superb responsiveness, another key attribute when conditions dictate constant throttle and brake inputs to maintain momentum and control. Both types of engine are fitted with an FIA-approved billet aluminium air restrictor, ensuring that all competitors are on a level playing field when it comes to engine power and that ability and set-up are more important than outright performance.

The Wildcat features front-mounted coolers for engine and transmission oil as well as power steering fluid, since all these areas will be working incredibly hard during the 15-day event. The engine cooling radiators are mounted in the rear compartment to protect them from potential damage.

Wheels and tyres

The team uses Cooper Tires Discoverer STT off-road tyres, mounted on Silverline Blindo wheels to offer unparalled grip, traction and durability – all vital for the assault on the Dakar Rally.

Cooper has an enviable reputation on the Dakar. In 2012 the brand won the Production Class, and the Discoverer STT is the most aggressive offering from the Cooper range. The construction of the tyre provides exceptional strength and damage resistance, while the large tread blocks generate incredible traction in gravel, mud and sand – all conditions that are encountered on the Dakar.

The Silverline Blindo wheels, which are cast in aluminium, are incredibly strong and light, meaning that they can withstand the demands of the event while keeping the vehicle's unsprung weight as low as possible. Low unsprung weight allows the suspension to react more quickly to changing surface conditions and keep the tyres in contact with the ground for the maximum amount of time, to the benefit of traction.

Because the Wildcat uses four-wheel drive, the Dakar regulations prohibit the use of on-board tyre pressure management systems. Therefore, if the crews need to change the tyre pressure, for example to increase grip in soft sand, they must let air out manually before re-inflating the tyres with the on-board air compressor.

Each Wildcat carries two spare wheels and tyres in case of punctures or damage on a special stage. Over the course of the event, the team were supported with 64 tyres and 12 spare wheel rims.

Transmission

The drive train is based on Land Rover designs but has been significantly strengthened to cope with the demands of the Dakar. Axle casings are reinforced to improve reliability and strength while bespoke high-strength half-shafts are fitted within the casings, to improve reliability and cope with the engine's performance as well as shock loadings – when wheels regain grip after slippery sections or following landings, for example.

Coupled to the transmission is the latest Quaife QBE86G Land Rover six-speed sequential gearbox. The use of a sequential gearbox has several benefits, not least the elimination of the need to use the clutch for every gearchange once the car is moving – essential for drivers with prosthetic legs. It also eliminates the chances of mis-shifts, which can be all too common, particularly in the heat of the moment and when bumping around in the desert. Instead of selecting gears using a traditional 'H' pattern, one pull back on the lever selects the next gear up; one push forward changes down.

Working in conjunction with the gearbox are Quaife ATB helical gear limited slip differentials, front and rear. These ensure that, even in situations of the lowest grip, the Wildcats are able to put the maximum torque, and hence traction, down on the surface. They are fitted with uprated Ashcroft crown wheels and pinions, again developed to handle the engine output as well as shock loads.

Brakes

The team uses high-performance Alcon brakes with 320mm vented and grooved discs with alloy calipers, giving the Wildcat racers the best capabilities in mixed driving conditions and terrains as well as exceptional durability. The vented discs allow heat to dissipate, while the grooves not only help to preserve the surface of the brake pads but also clear debris, such as sand, away from the pad area and ensure optimum braking performance at all times.

The calipers are a four-piston design front and rear and are drilled internally for fluid transfer. This means that other than the fluid flexible pipe, there are no external connections that could become damaged and, at best, require repair, or at worst, cause an accident. The calipers are designed to accept 28mm pads; these are thicker than traditional motorsport brake pads to reflect the huge mileages that the Wildcats will need to cover between the team service area in the overnight bivouacs.

Instrumentation

Information is key on an event like the Dakar and the on-board instrumentation system from PowerStation and Bosch keeps the driver and co-driver informed of the state of the vehicle at all times. Traditional information such as engine, transmission and oil temperatures are displayed, while the dash also features a gear read-out for the sequential transmission. Vehicles are individually tailored to suit the crew; for example, the car driven by Tony Harris features a sensor on the clutch pedal to indicate if he is riding the clutch, since he cannot feel pressure through his prosthetic left leg.

The co-drivers have a vast array of information to monitor and take in. They will be reading the road book – mounted on to a powered motorcycle rolling display in Tom Neathway's case – as well as the GPS IriTrack navigation unit, to ensure that they hit every waypoint on the route. They will also be keeping a close eye on the twin Terratrip trip computers to ensure they know exactly where they are at all times.

All four Wildcats are fitted with a 3M Peltor intercom system, allowing the crew to communicate comfortably in even the most hostile environments. Externally, each car is fitted with a selection of driving lights from the Lazer Lamps range. There are again two benefits here: they provide illumination in case the cars have to complete their stages at night and they also alert other competitors, officials, spectators and locals of the car's approach.

Hydraulic self-jacking system

The Wildcat features a unique advantage over its competitors with its on-board self-jacking system.

A hydraulic ram forces a skid plate down underneath the car which is capable of lifting the Wildcat's wheels and tyres off the ground completely. Not only does this make wheel changes easier, it also means that the Wildcat can lift itself out of sticky situations and get itself going again.

Typically, in soft, dry sand the jack can help 'walk' the car out of trouble by lifting the wheels and allowing sand to flow back into the hole that is left. If this is not enough, then the crew can generally use the lift to get at least one sand ladder under a wheel to drag themselves out.

Seats and harnesses

Driving over sand dunes or rocky tracks for 16 hours a day means the seats and harnesses must be designed for the task. They need to be comfortable, supportive and safe in case the car is involved in an accident. Similarly, the harnesses need to be adjustable yet strong enough to secure the occupant. These tasks are performed admirably by Corbeau seats and Luke harnesses, while Luke also supplied the various straps and tie-downs used on the vehicles to secure spare wheels and tyres, tools, rescue equipment and so on.

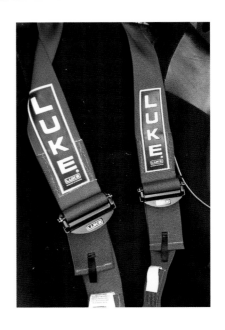

SPECIFICATION

Race weight	13 tonnes
Length	6.5m
Width	2.5m
Wheelbase	3.8m
Approach angle	55 degrees
Departure angle	58 degrees
Break over	140 degrees
Max gradient	1 in 1
Side slope	40 degrees

While often ungainly, the trucks in the T4 class in general, and the Race2Recovery team's Renault Kerax in particular, are spectacular vehicles – and superbly equipped to tackle the route. With their huge ground clearance, four-wheel drive, 16-speed transmission and more than 1,800lb/ft of torque (the equivalent of six Wildcats), they can navigate almost any terrain. Prepared by HMS Engineering and XCeed Motorsport, the team's Kerax truck uses Fox Racing shock absorbers and the body houses a fully functioning mobile workshop, with parts and tools carefully tied down while in action.

The Kerax features the same navigation equipment as the Wildcats – twin trip computers and the GPS IriTrack system – and carries three crew members (driver, co-driver and riding mechanic) who, for communication on the move, use a three-way version of the same Peltor intercoms used in the Wildcats.

← The Renault Kerax carries three crew – driver, navigator and mechanic

'The Interceptor', as the Renault Kerax 4x4 truck is known, is a racer through and through, intended to support the T1 Wildcats on the special stages that make up the Dakar, following the same route and competing in the T4 category. The truck supports the Wildcats with a larger array of spare parts and tools than they can carry themselves, and can even recover a car if it cannot continue on its own.

'The Duff'

The Daf Drops 8x8 was prepared by Xceed Motorsport, while its box body was developed to the team's bespoke design by Qlog and Partumis Metal. The body is based on a shipping container, but with many modifications. The container was mounted to a drop sled while the lifting structure at the front was fabricated. One side was cut out and replaced with a fold-up roof. Internally, a series of racks and workbenches was created to allow not only safe and secure storage but a weatherproof and efficient workspace. The conversion took just four weeks!

The body taking shape. Here you can see the flip-up side panel

The team's two T5 trucks are based on an eight-wheel-drive (8x8) chassis and equipped with a demountable, or Drops, body. While many other teams use similar trucks (but with the body remaining in place on the chassis), the adoption of the two Drops boxes means that the disabled team members can access all facilities in the T5s easily, quickly and safely.

Man Kat

The Man Kat 8x8, provided by Quin Evans and Ben Gott, has completed more Dakars than most, having been used on previous occasions to support various competitors, including works teams. Its military Drops design allows the box body to be dropped to ground level in less than two minutes. The Man Kat box contains a selection of tools and parts, but is aimed more at supporting the team members, with a shower, on-board generator to run the entire team bivouac, a bed for the driver to get some rest on long liaison sections, and even a washing machine!

⬈ The MAN Kat has her own fan base!

SUPPORT CARS

Land Rover is supporting the team with two Discoveries and one Defender 130 – vehicles that are perfectly suited to the harsh desert dunes, arid tracks, high altitudes and arduous terrain found on the Dakar Rally.

These three vehicles carry team personnel, including mechanics, between bivouacs (overnight stops) along the same route as the two T5 trucks, allowing mechanics in particular to rest in between bivouacs to ensure they're ready for whatever tasks await them at the end of each competitive day. The cars are known by their call signs: team management travel in 'Green Leader' (Discovery) while the mechanics are split between 'Slider' (Discovery) and 'Lazy Boy' (Defender 130).

Land Rover's support of Race2Recovery has also included the supply of Land Rover engines for use in the team's race vehicles, off-road driving training, a favourable spares and parts supply arrangement, plus PR, marketing and financial support. The provision and funding of these resources assisted the team's logistical and management tasks that would otherwise have required a major outlay of funds.

RACE2RECOVERY
THE TRAINING

> *'Sand driving — specifically negotiating sand dunes, ergs and razor-back features — is one of the most difficult terrains to master; traction and vehicle control will change over a few metres and through the day.'*
>
> **Mark Cullum, Race2Recovery off-road driving instructor**

RACE2RECOVERY
SAND DUNE TRAINING

Before members of the team jetted off to Morocco for sand dune training in October 2012, initial training sessions were arranged in the UK by Mark Cullum, off-road driving instructor and team member, at a site on the North Devon coast that offered dunes with major ascents and descents on soft coastal sand, to replicate the dunes of the Dakar.

'Sand driving – and specifically negotiating sand dunes, ergs and razor-back features – is one of the most difficult and challenging terrains to master,' explained Mark. 'Traction and ultimately vehicle control in sand will change over a few metres and through the day. Crossing a set of sand seas and dunes in the morning will be much easier than during the late afternoon when the sun has reduced the surface tension and therefore grip.'

The training site in Devon was a great opportunity for the guys to hone basic skills in sand driving, but ultimately the team needed to experience the real desert and its arid terrain, which is why the time spent training in Morocco was vital. The racing pairs took part and the trip was organised by Mark Cullum and a team from Land Rover's off-road Experience.

The original plan had been to take part in the Rallye de Maroc, but due to lack of funding a week of intense training took its place and was actually just as valuable. Mark had the lads up early and learning from the moment they opened their eyes. They trained in three Land Rover Defender 110s on rocky terrain, scree slopes, subca (early formation of rock), and on small and large sand dunes, not forgetting the long-distance journeys in between all this terrain to get to their destinations. The long distances, sometimes up to 1,000km, were ideal opportunities to practise speed control; on the Dakar there are many sections where speed limits apply.

⬇ **Dunes in Morocco stretch to the horizon: the Defender 110 was the perfect training vehicle**

'You need discipline and you need to maximise your concentration and stamina,' explained Tony Harris, after a long trek towards the Algerian border where they met some conspicuous-looking security guards dressed in dodgy Barcelona football shirts! 'These factors are especially important when you have been driving for close to 12 hours. That's when things go wrong and you can get sloppy.'

Mark worked the team hard and several vital messages were drummed into them during the Morocco training. For example, not following in each other's tracks; although this might seem a logical thing to do, churned-up sand provides less traction for the vehicle behind. Also, when driving on small sand dunes, avoid cresting them the wrong way as there are two sides to a dune; the windward side is the side to ascend as the sand is compact, while the leeward side, where the sand is loose, is the side to descend.

'We were relearning all the time,' explained Gareth Paterson, 'Mark really did put us through our paces and we had to undo a lot of bad habits. Just a quick one for you: when you deflate your tyres to increase traction, we thought it was to increase the width of the tyre but. no, you want to increase the length instead. See, I was listening in class!'

ICE DRIVING

In February 2012 a trip to Norway was organised. Is ice driving relevant to preparing for the dunes of the Dakar? Yes, more than anyone could imagine! Tony Harris, Ben Gott, Gareth Paterson and Sean Whatley spent three days near Oslo, pounding the ice in Porsches as well as 4x4s.

'The beauty of ice is it's a lot safer,' explained Tony. 'If you make a mistake, you just slide; there's no rolling. Ice accentuates your strengths and weaknesses, and any driver training you can do is beneficial.'

When the guys arrived in Norway there was meant to be ice as far as the eye could see. However, a freak heat wave had hit the country and there were concerns the ice would not be thick enough. A morning was spent tapping the ice and gingerly walking over its surface, but luckily the four still managed to take part in two and a half days of training.

Mark Cullum came on board just in time... 'Their rallying experience in the UK hadn't offered the opportunity to grasp the basics of vehicle design, traction enhancement systems, suspension limitations and clearance factors when operating vehicles over varying terrain conditions.'

The big dune training was what the guys had been waiting for. After taking it slowly over the subca, the 'yellow jaws' were soon upon them. Tony Harris: 'It was easy to see who was taking to it naturally and who needed a bit more help. Appreciating the gears and using them instead of the clutch was very useful, as the clutch can easily be burnt out in an event like the Dakar – and a clutch isn't cheap to replace.

⇐ **Mark Cullum used the simplest of models coupled with practical demonstrations to impart his wisdom**

The training took part in some very remote areas with not an animal, let alone a human being, in sight for hundreds of miles. It was, of course, impossible to find a hotel with mod cons in such an area, so the crew had to spend the night camping with no gear. 'I slept on the roof of one of the cars with my head wedged between two shovels to stop me rolling off in the middle of the night,' laughed Barney Gillespie. 'It's true that a few unorthodox sleeping positions were adopted, but it was one way of getting to know each other a bit better!'

The film crew were never far away, capturing every move and mistake, but one night their film equipment couldn't be charged due to lack of electrical facilities. Another time the film crew's Discovery suffered two punctures so the other cars had to waste valuable time repairing them. It was yet another lesson about organisation, communication and working in pairs.

Refuelling and supplies were needed for the journey home, so a stop for some bread and cheese was popular. A trip of 800km to the hotel was next on the list and the journey took the cars through some mind-blowing landscapes, including mountains, vineyards,

⬇ **Tony Harris guns the power to crest the dune without burning the clutch!**

↑ The team of rally pioneers circle their wagons for the night

↓ Practising complicated recoveries

arid desert and olive groves, before finally ending up on the coast where the beers were waiting. Matt O'Hare had a close shave a few miles from the hotel – a local driver decided to stop in the dust with no warning and no brake lights – but he managed to stop a foot before the clapped-out bumper. It was just one more flash of excitement before catching the EasyJet flight from Marrakech to London Gatwick, on an Airbus A320 registered G-EZUS. Yes, you read that correctly!

The guys couldn't get enough, so four more days of sand training were organised for December 2012 in the Atlas Mountains. This time the racing pairs were faced with much bigger dunes and, unlike the first time around, the drivers and navigators were paired together when tackling the terrain, as they would be on the real rally.

It was hard for the drivers not be distracted by the stunning landscape, but they were there to learn and they kept their minds focused – for the most part. Matt's concentration lapsed once when he pulled away from a stop and hit a drain, but he wasn't the only one who made a mistake, because Tony managed to park his Defender in a snowdrift and got royally stuck!

⬆ Cathy Derousseaux watches as Tony Harris
shovels the Sahara out of his foot

⬇ Tony gets a hand
out of the white stuff

RACE2RECOVERY
NAVIGATION TRAINING

It's not just the drivers who had to go back to school. The navigators needed some training too. Navigators are crucial for a successful rally and their roles are varied and complicated. Twelve hours in a hot car with another person isn't always a perfect recipe for harmony, however, and has even been described as being much like a marriage.

Although Quin Evans had to leave the racing pairs due to family commitments, his knowledge and experience were resources that couldn't be left untapped. He stayed on as part of the support team (and latterly Team Principal Advisor), offering his services in a training role.

'To be a good navigator, you mustn't suffer from car sickness. That's the first priority!' says Quin. 'Your sense of direction must be impeccable, and you must be unflappable. It's your job to see potential accidents before they happen but not to worry the driver unnecessarily.'

Quin covered everything that the navigators would need out on the Dakar, from handy items like a scarf (good for cleaning and during sandstorms), sun cream and a toilet roll, to the important equipment needed in the cockpit such as maps of day routes, a road book and goggles. He also highlighted how the different types of sand should be tackled. For example, flat plains (also known as chotts) are attacked in a very different way from dunes.

↑ **Tom Neathway in his element with the latest navigating gadgets**

← **Quin Evans explains the importance of tyre pressures to the navigators**

Navigating over chotts:

- Usually taken at a fast speed, but it's difficult to see cautions and detours;
- There are lots of bumps that kick up the back end of the vehicle;
- Sometimes it's tricky to climb out of a chott at the right place.

Navigating over dunes:

- Always stay as high as you can;
- Do not encourage local help if you get stuck – always rely on fellow competitors;
- Never stop at a low point;
- Do not get led by crowds.

In-car routine has to be strictly followed by the navigator and includes looking after the driver throughout a stage:

- Mark in the road book regular instrument checks, regular feeds and drinks (and insist on all this for the driver);
- Explain the coming terrain in sections to the driver;
- Establish if any communication is required with the rest of the team;
- Write down any issues as they happen;
- If you see a cameraman, slow down – the number one rule of all!

⬆ **Mark Cullum goes over the route one last time**

'Your sense of direction must be impeccable, and you must be unflappable. It's your job to see potential accidents before they happen but not to worry the driver unnecessarily.'

Quin Evans, navigator trainer

RACE2RECOVERY
SAFETY TRAINING

There was no escaping the treadmills, oxygen masks and endless fitness programmes, but what was just as important was first aid, fire and extraction training. Dave Marsh, who has spent over 25 years in the fire service, set up a vital weekend of training to cover all three of these crucial areas for the whole team.

After Tom Neathway and Dave suffered a roll in the Tuareg Rally that saw their car end up on its side, they both realised that getting a car upright again – hard enough with two able-bodied people – was impossible because triple amputee Tom couldn't assist... and what would have happened if his co-driver had been knocked out by the impact

⬆ Matt and Charles learn how to use fire extinguishers correctly

⬇ Pav discusses the extraction exercise with amputees Tom and Tony

↑ The team
with the Devon
& Somerset
Fire Service
and Ambulance
technicians

→ Tom cuts his
way from the
vehicle using a
Bosch powersaw

→ Tom practising
CPR

⬆ Tony inserting an airway in the confines of the Wildcat cabin

↗ Triple Amputee Tom Neathway receives his crash vehicle self extraction certificate

➜ Barney and Tom feel the pressure as they prepare for emergency situations on the Dakar

and both had been trapped? Each car has as much as 375 litres of petrol on board and isn't the place to be stuck with the risk of fire never far away.

'The Devon and Somerset Fire Service were brilliant,' said Dave. 'They were more than happy to help us out and everyone got lots from the two days. We combined it with first aid and extraction sessions so we were now fully prepared if the worst was to happen. The Chief Medical Officer at the

MSA (Motor Sports Association) was impressed with our commitment and we showed him how serious we were about doing the event properly. He was happy to approve Tom's Class A international cross-country race licence, which at the time was a first for a triple amputee.'

PERSONAL TRAINING

Paul White, the training advisor, has over 25 years of experience in extreme sports, from working with Formula 1 drivers to teams that have broken world records rowing the Atlantic and conquering uncharted peaks in the Arctic Circle.

'When I met the team in June 2012 I explained to them that, due to the time restraints, I would endeavour to do the simple things with excellence rather than take on the whole subject of human performance and under-deliver on outcomes,' Paul explained. 'My first move was to establish a team of experts to assist me in this challenge. I chose Bernie Shrosbree, personal trainer to Formula 1 driver Mark Webber, who has been a close friend in many of the adventures I have taken part in, and Dr Andy Middlebrooke, a sports scientist and principal of Exercise Science Consulting.'

Under the watchful eyes of Paul, Andy and Bernie, the guys benefited from expert advice on nutrition, hydration and physical performance in the build-up to the Dakar. Being lads from the services, the advice to head to the gym and treat the body like a temple wasn't always rigorously adhered to, and families and jobs often had to take priority. However, Paul, Andy and Bernie worked hard with the team and after just three short months, towards the end of 2012, they were as ready as they were ever going to be. They'd also found muscles they never knew they had!

'After doing a VO2 max test on the treadmill, I thought my life was over!' said Dave Marsh. 'You basically run for as long as you can while the speed of the treadmill creeps up every minute – it's totally exhausting and something I never want to do again. Saying that, Paul pushed me as far as I could go and I was pleased with where that was, as I'm not as young as I used to be. I wasn't sick either, which was a relief; the others did warn me about that.'

No living creature can survive without adequate hydration or the right nutrition for the task. This area was crucial for Paul White and his team to get right, as without taking on the correct liquid and food, illness and loss of concentration can take hold and become key disaster areas for any extreme sports team. It is well documented by Dakar doctors that if riders and drivers paid more attention to these areas, some serious accidents and even fatalities could have been avoided. Armed with this information, Karl Bingley at USN Nutrition and Hydration Products was quickly on Paul's speed dial and they worked up a suitable package of nutrition between them. The guys then spent an invaluable day learning how to hydrate and feed themselves properly on the Dakar.

For the Dakar itself, drivers and navigators were given a day sack containing nutritional gels, protein bars, water bottle (pure water as you cannot risk tap water contaminants), enhanced dietary supplement tablets and a multi-nutritional gel; all of these are designed to enhance the performance and endurance of team members by restoring fluid and electrolytes, replenishing glycogen, reducing muscle and immune stress, and aid in rebuilding muscle protein. On altitude stages a VO2 tablet can also be taken to increase oxygen uptake and reduce muscle pain and stiffness. Cathy Derousseaux even opted to bring some of her own pure oxygen canisters in case of need.

Ignoring just one supplement can reduce personal performance by as much as 30%, which can contribute to the difference between retiring or continuing on the Dakar. The gels were also recommended for mechanics after any big physical job on a car as they could expel as much energy as the racing pairs.

'I knew from the outset,' concludes Paul, 'that I wouldn't be able to maximise the team's ability to cover all areas of human performance, due to the lads being scattered all over the country and the fact that we didn't have the luxury of running as a full-time professional team. However, the key objectives were to establish a good immediate understanding of the race team's fitness levels, build a sound hydration system on to the cars and trucks, train the team to understand the consequences of not hydrating and feeding properly, and work with Pav to iron out some of the day-to-day emotional issues that affect a team's performance.'

RACE2RECOVERY
SIMULATOR TRAINING

John Winskill, T4 team member and director at Boeing Defence UK Ltd, rose to the challenge (along with a group from his office) of supporting the team by providing unlimited access to their state-of-the-art advanced simulation facility called 'The Portal'.

Based in Fleet, Hampshire, this facility is specifically designed to test new concepts, and review and make decisions on current defence and security capabilities.

In support of Race2Recovery, the Boeing simulation engineers created two synthetic environments to help train the T1 racing pairs. They used the latest virtual simulation technologies, in association with Bohemia Interactive (UK) Ltd, to project the navigators' view through the window of the race Wildcat on to a 200sq ft HD (high-definition) screen – very much like an IMAX.

⬆ **The navigators watch the simulator's 200sq ft screen**

This real-time virtual simulation enabled the navigators to work through their road books in groups while looking out of a virtual T1 race car being driven by a computer-simulated driver. The technology helped the navigators to run a road-book route in exactly the same manner as they would do on the Dakar, but also to stop and play back their routes as many times as they felt necessary in order to learn from errors or adjust their processes – and all in the safety of a simulated race vehicle.

Once they'd established their processes as a group, the navigators were then taken to the second simulator. This was based on a T1 race car chassis with a through-the-windscreen view of the terrain ahead. In this simulator, an individual navigator is able to sit with their driver and practise the techniques and procedures learned in the large auditorium, working up the skills that would be needed during the race with their driver on a one-to-one basis.

Using the race team's Peltor helmets, the Boeing engineers were able to replicate all the sounds, bumps, creaks and vibrations of the race vehicle at high speed, as well as the internal intercom that is so critical to both driver and navigator. Boeing's

Apache attack helicopter technologies were also used to modify the helmets to provide a realistic soundtrack to the simulator's representations of the racing environment.

Race-team simulation is not just the pre-requisite of the big Formula 1 teams. Helped by Boeing engineers (largely in their own time), the Race2Recovery racing pairs had the opportunity to prepare really well for the Dakar Rally.

⬆ **A Wildcat cabin was fitted into a container with the electronics to create a realistic simulator**

⬇ **Justin Birchall gets to grips with the simulator**

RACE2RECOVERY
FIRST OUTINGS

'The entire motorsport community and fans made us feel so welcome and the support we had was truly humbling.'

Tony Harris on Race2Recovery's appearance at the Goodwood Festival of Speed 2012

RACE2RECOVERY
COMPETITIVE OUTINGS

During 2011 and 2012 Race2Recovery team members participated in various rallying events, both in the UK and abroad, all with the ultimate goal of everyone securing their International Cross Country Licences. This type of licence (or an International Rally Licence) is needed to compete in the Dakar Rally – and to obtain one requires starting at the bottom of the ladder.

The novice's licence is a Non-Race Clubman or Rally National B licence, provided by the Motor Sports Association (MSA), the UK motorsport federation, designated by the world governing body, the Fédération Internationale de l'Automobile (FIA). Either licence allows a beginner to compete in clubman events, with the target of finishing four rallies (which is harder than it sounds) before he or she is allowed to upgrade to the next level.

With the exception of Justin Birchall, Ben Gott

⬆ **The Ray Kempster Memorial Rally was one of the events where team members began honing their skills**

⬇ **The team, with Freelander, at their first British Cross Country Championship race in 2011**

and Chris Ratter, all the competing members of Race2Recovery needed to start from scratch – and with only a single car available to begin with, this was a feat in its own right. However, in the true spirit of the project, many other teams and drivers helped enormously by allowing members to sit in and gain the necessary signatures.

Once each member had amassed four signatures on their National B licence, the next challenge was to upgrade to a National A licence, which meant completing two more events at this level before being eligible to apply for an International Licence. Part of that process includes a full medical, with a resting ECG trace for drivers under 45 and a treadmill test with a consultant's report for those over that age.

Race2Recovery started competing in 2011 with a single Land Rover Freelander in the Marches 4×4 British Cross Country Championship (BCCC) and immediately began gaining the experience and skills they would need on the Dakar. The BCCC is a hotly fought series of six events held throughout the country. Contested by some of Britain's finest off-road racers, it is more demanding than people first imagine, sporting cars with supercharged engines, uprated suspension and enormous grip, and resulting in

some truly amazing action. As the 2011 season drew to a close, Race2Recovery also took to their restricted 275bhp Wildcats, the vehicles they would actually use on the Tuareg and Dakar rallies, for the first time since appearing on *Top Gear* that summer.

February 2012 saw the team step up another gear with their first international outing, in North Africa on the Tuareg Rallye, which is covered in detail in the next chapter. This was also their first experience of an International Rally Raid and of competing on sand dunes. Here, the learning curve became almost vertical as they proved the team's mantra 'Beyond Injury, Achieving the Extraordinary', but both car that were entered reached the finish, the one crewed by Dave Marsh and Tom Neathway achieving a solid 10th place result. This set the scene for the rest of the year, as the team continued to compete in the BCCC and approach the Dakar entry deadline.

⬆ **Early days: the team used a Land Rover Freelander of standard specification (except for safety modifications) in the British Cross Country Championship**

Britpart Freelander Challenge

The team gained the majority of their experience and began building the R2R publicity machine by participating in the Britpart Freelander Challenge class of the BCCC. This series comprises any four of the six published BCCC events and is designed to encourage newcomers into the sport of cross-country racing, as the Freelanders used are based on standard production vehicles. The only modifications are the addition of the safety features required to comply with the MSA regulations.

As the series runs parallel with the BCCC, it allowed the team to compete in a relatively inexpensive car – suitable race-ready Freelanders are about £5,000 while donor cars, to use as a base for bespoke builds, start from £500. Compare that with around £50,000 for a second-hand Wildcat!

On their first outing in Scotland, on the Borders Hill Rally, the team began gaining experience but, unfortunately, not the sort they were hoping for. Flying rocks damaged the oil filter on the Freelander's

engine and it lost all of its oil, leading to catastrophic, and terminal, failure.

A replacement donor vehicle wasn't easy to find – it had to be exactly the same specification as the original – but after many hours spent browsing the internet and making telephone calls one was found, with a good engine but a damaged gearbox.

↑ Britpart Freelander Challenge is incredibly cost-effective, using standard Land Rover Freelanders as an introduction to off-road racing

ARMED FORCES RALLY TEAM

The famous Armed Forces Rally Team has assisted Race2Recovery hugely in a number of ways on events over the past two years. This non-profit-making, tri-service organisation is the pinnacle for team motorsport within the combined forces, and all advanced drivers from the Royal Navy, Army and Royal Air Force aspire to be part of it.

The Armed Forces Rally Team competes in the National category of several events on the British Rally Championship (BRC) each year, as well as in the National class of the British round of the FIA World Rally Championship and Rally Reykjavik in Iceland. Each event includes several different classes; the Armed Forces Rally Team competes in the Land Rover class. As for the Race2Recovery team, they gained vital cross-country experience behind the wheel of the Land Rover Defender Wolf 300TDi at events in the UK such as Wales Rally GB.

The mechanic team descended on Dave Reeve's home for the weekend, put up tents in the garden, squeezed into his tiny workshop and got to work swapping the broken engine for the replacement. After a productive first day, a well-earned barbecue and a few beers provided a welcome time-out. 'Barney' Gillespie was a little too relaxed, though, and at breakfast he couldn't find his prosthetic leg. Dave's son James, wandering into the bathroom, had the shock of his life to find a leg, complete with sock and shoe, leaning against the bath. Recovering from his surprise he came downstairs, asking, 'Has anyone lost a leg?'

Sunday saw the team working with full focus to get the car running by the end of the day, and when it finally fired up there was a huge cheer. As people had to gradually leave for work commitments the next day, Sean Whatley and Dave worked on to make the final connections and get the job finished. The trusty Freelander was back in action.

The team ran the Freelander throughout the 2011 and 2012 seasons with a number of drivers and co-drivers to make sure everyone got their necessary licences. Due to the number of signatures required, and only six rounds in the BCCC in each season,

a number of other events were needed including the National category of Wales Rally GB in 2011, which was not only good publicity for the R2R guys but also gave them an opportunity to see how some of the professional teams and drivers worked.

⬇ Nikki Paterson, with trusty Haynes Manual on standby, helps with Freelander engine rebuild

RACE2RECOVERY
PROMOTIONAL OUTINGS

Appearing before the public and being available to chat to the press, supporters and fans is vital for any charity, and especially so for Race2Recovery. People can then begin to understand its overall aims and feel part of the endeavour, not only by donating money but also by following the daily twists and turns in the build-up to the big event. The team began appearing in public in the autumn of 2011. Then almost every weekend in 2012, particularly throughout the summer months, was taken up with public appearances all over the UK, from the world-renowned Goodwood Festival of Speed in Sussex to one-off appearances at centres for disabled and injured patients.

BBC TV's *Top Gear*
August 2011

Members of Race2Recovery were first noticed by the public after *Top Gear* filmed them as part of the 'Project Mobility' piece. Presenter Richard Hammond attended a round of the BCCC where team members were trying out a Wildcat for the first time and was immediately impressed with their approach, outlook and determination. One crucial aspect for the team was the support of its first patron, Ben Collins, the former 'Stig' from the show. His experience coaching not only 'Stars in a Reasonably Priced Car' but as a stunt driver for Hollywood blockbusters, as well as tactical driving instruction for branches of the military, would prove invaluable.

Following filming of the piece early in 2011, where Tony Harris and Tom Neathway were seen competing together in the Wildcat, Race2Recovery was formed with the intention of becoming the first disabled team to compete in the Dakar Rally and, in the process, raise money for key service charities and inspire the wider disabled community. The *Top Gear* appearance was a perfect launch pad for the campaign.

⬇ The team's first major public appearance was at Rallyday in 2011 when it ran the Orange Plant Wildcat for the first time

Rallyday

Castle Combe, September 2011

Rallyday at Castle Combe is a big draw for all rally fans, and with support from organisers Brian Stubbings, Darin Frow and Simon Miskelly, the team offered members of the public the thrill of a Wildcat ride to help raise funds for the charity. The team was delighted to be given two passenger rides to auction for charity – one with Matthew Wilson in the Ford Fiesta World Rally Championship car and the other with Harri Rovanperä in the MML Sports Mitsubishi Lancer EvoX R4 car.

TeamSport Karting

London Bridge, October 2011

The team was thrilled when TeamSport invited them to race alongside Nick Hamilton at its London Bridge indoor karting centre, for the launch of its new electric karts and hand controls for disabled racers. Despite Nick's obvious training and pedigree – he competes successfully in the Renault Clio Cup series which supports the British Touring Car Championship – Tom Neathway, in his hand-controlled kart, gave him a serious run for his money, finishing less than a second adrift in the final race.

↑ The team with Nick Hamilton at the TeamSport track at London Bridge

← Tom Neathway was immediately on the pace in his hand-controlled electric kart

Autosport International

Birmingham NEC, January 2012

This was the team's first major public appearance and it took place at the annual Autosport International show, widely regarded as the world's leading motorsport exhibition and the launch pad for many team and manufacturer motorsport programmes. Race2Recovery was hardly a household name at this time, but that definitely began to change during the exhibition. The crowds were in awe of the Wildcat, power-sliding and jumping in the Live Action Arena, and Tony Harris was on hand to build up the atmosphere and excitement. Whatever he did worked wonders, as the team raised £15,000 just by rattling six buckets.

→ The team made its presence known in the Live Action Arena of Autosport International at the NEC for three days in January 2012

➜ The Ratcat appeared on the Alcon stand throughout the Autosport International show

➜➜ Tony Harris and Tom Neathway with the Wildcat and two highly visible fans at BBC Media City the day before the Pageant of Power

Disability Day

Stoke-on-Trent, April 2012

This one-day event was held at Stoke-on-Trent Sixth Form College. It was a relatively low-key function, as none of the team cars was present, but days like this, as Team Manager 'Pav' Taylor explained, are just as important as the higher-profile public events such as Goodwood Festival of Speed.

Pageant of Power

Cholmondeley Castle, Cheshire June 2012

The majority of the team attended this three-day event with one of the Wildcats in the stunning grounds of Cholmondeley Castle. The relatively young Pageant of Power brings together some of the highest-octane action on land, air and water, and was a great success for the team, with amazing support from fans and the general public. The Wildcat was put through its paces as excited visitors took passenger rides around a circuit where the huge amount of mud couldn't dampen their spirits.

The day before the pageant, Tony Harris and Tom Neathway had gone to the BBC's Media City in Salford and were interviewed on Radio Manchester. The R2R team then formed part of the procession to the event, which officially opened the proceedings.

⬇ Despite the typical British summer weather, the Wildcat rides raised pulses and a huge amount of money for the charity

Goodwood Festival of Speed

28 June to 1 July 2012

In the build-up to the world-famous Goodwood Festival of Speed the team proudly announced its partnership with Land Rover, who would be their major sponsor. The iconic British marque would go on to provide vehicle and parts support, as well as invaluable bespoke desert training.

All the team personnel attended this major event, and they were split across three distinct areas. Several Wildcats gave demonstration runs through the Forest Rally Stage, while the team also had a presence in the main arena, where visitors could find out more about the team and its members, sip champagne (to raise funds), donate to the cause and purchase Race2Recovery merchandise.

However, by far the most interesting area for visitors was the 'Dakar Experience', set up near the Formula 1 paddock, where fans were given the opportunity to experience at first hand some of the pressures and demands that the most arduous motorsport adventure in the world would place on team personnel. Race2Recovery ran a wheel-change competition with a *Top Gear*-style leaderboard, where members of the public could try their hand at changing one of the Silverline wheels and Cooper Tires rubber that the team was using on its Wildcats. Each daily winner went on to enjoy a ride in one of the Wildcats on the Forest Stage.

The competition was a definite draw not only for the public but also for the mechanics of the Ferrari Formula 1 team, who notched up an impressive 38 seconds. However, Race2Recovery's mechanic and storeman, Gareth Paterson, posted a blistering 32 seconds and seriously impressed the Italians.

The following day, the Ferrari team repaid the favour, inviting Gareth to experience changing a tyre on an F2012 Formula 1 car – in 2.0 seconds. Gareth posted an impressive 4.5 seconds – not bad for a first attempt.

The Race2Recovery guys also enjoyed meeting personalities from the motorsport world, including 2009 Dakar winner Giniel de Villiers, McLaren boss Ron Dennis and Red Bull Racing's Formula 1 driver Mark Webber, who was later photographed sporting a Race2Recovery wristband.

Drivers Dave Marsh and Tony Harris seized the opportunity to tackle the world-famous hill climb in the Wildcats, but it was Ben Gott, Martyn Williams

← The 'Dakar Experience' wheel-change competition at Goodwood proved a huge hit, with visitors and fans, as well as…

← …the Ferrari Formula 1 mechanics, who were only just slower than R2R's Gareth Paterson

↓ The following day, Gareth tried his hand on Ferrari's F2012 F1 car. Smaller wheels and tyres, more hands, much less time…

→ The Wildcats proved hugely popular at Goodwood as they ran up the famous hill-climb course...

↓ ...but the Man Kat 8x8 truck was the largest vehicle ever to have tackled the hill; it only just fitted under the footbridge across the track

and Charles Sincock who stole the show, taking the team's Man Kat 8x8 T5 support truck on the course to rousing applause from the crowds. The height of both the footbridge and the truck had to be carefully evaluated before the largest-ever vehicle to climb the hill was released.

'The entire motorsport community and fans made us feel so welcome and the support we had was truly humbling,' Tony said afterwards.

Rallyday
Castle Combe, August 2012

In August 2012 the team returned to Rallyday for another action-packed event that was full of fun but also had a few sticky moments...

The Renault Kerax T4 truck opened proceedings, followed on to the circuit by three of the team's Wildcats. Once again the organisers allowed the R2R guys to 'sell' passenger rides on the off-road course

to raise money, but Tony somehow managed to roll his car as the crowd looked on, much to the delight of his fellow team members. Thankfully, he walked away unscathed and blamed it squarely on mechanical failure! Unfortunately, the engine turned out to be terminally damaged; it was very embarrassing for everyone, but best for it to happen then and not out in the dunes.

Regent Street Car Show
London, November 2012

This event was more concerned with raising the profile of R2R than about money, and was one of the last opportunities the team had to catch the public's eye before they headed off for the Dakar itself. The team displayed the I.R.D. Wildcat and this provided a great opportunity for interviews and for chatting with fans and supporters.

⬇ Regent Street has rarely been this quiet; needless to say, it didn't remain so once the Wildcat fired up

INSPIRED TO RAISE MONEY

Race2Recovery has inspired many people to raise money for the charity and here are a few of the many personal stories.

➔ Pete Garlick, a long-time Race2Recovery supporter, walked 150 miles from Qt Services in Plymouth to Tedworth House in Tidworth, Wiltshire in September 2012, raising a magnificent £1,728.

➔ Claire Todd organised a Summer Ball at the Ross Park Hotel in Ballymena, Co. Antrim, in July 2012. A friend of Race2Recovery's Phillip 'Barney' Gillespie (pictured with some of the guests), Claire raised a splendid £2,200 and has since organised more fundraisers.

➔ Rich and Sarah Mitchell asked for donations to Race2Recovery instead of wedding gifts when they married on 10 August 2012 and were touched by everyone's kindness and generosity.

➔ Lisa Minto, Finance Manager at Race2Recovery sponsor Orange Plant, raised a fantastic £500 for the charity by competing in the 13-mile Great North Run in 2012, finishing in 2 hours 10 minutes.

➔ Rose Vivaciou and her friend Chris Baughurst took just over 20 hours to walk the 28 miles from Brighton to Bexhill on 2 June 2012, raising £200 for Race2Recovery; here Rose pauses to admire the Seven Sisters cliffs.

➔ Stephanie Boddez contracted meningitis when she was 18 and had to have both her legs amputated as a result. She struggled to cope, not knowing if she'd be able go to college or even drive a car – and she felt that no-one understood. Then she saw Tony Harris and Tom Neathway on *Top Gear* and that gave her a glimmer of hope. She emailed the team to thank them for inspiring her, kept in touch via Facebook and then, walking on her prosthetic legs, met the guys at the Goodwood Festival of Speed 2012 in July and had a ride in a Wildcat. The smile on Stephanie's face says it all, and the team felt honoured to have played a small part in her recovery.

'It was a real eye-opener – a big step up from doing a weekend rally to eight full-on days of driving. There were also lots of repairs needed on the cars after each day of racing so that limited the amount of rest.'

Andrew 'Pav' Taylor, Team Manager

RACE2RECOVERY
TUAREG RALLYE

Early in 2012, the team's programme and training accelerated rapidly. In order to develop their skills and experience in the type of conditions expected on the Dakar, a series of training and international rallies was added to their already busy calendar of fundraising opportunities and appearances at corporate events, not forgetting holding down full-time jobs and spending time with their families. Their first international outing was in March on the Tuareg Rallye in North Africa.

The Tuareg Rallye was founded by Rainer Autenrieth in 1999 and caters for everyone from absolute off-road beginners to Dakar pros. The first rally was staged in November of that year; the entry numbers were somewhat smaller then, with only two 4x4s and 15 motorcycles taking part in that first event. In 2012, 110 4x4s and 135 motorcycles took on the challenge, including two Race2Recovery

entries. For our guys it was the perfect opportunity to get some real training on a real African desert rally: Atlas Mountain trails; dry, rocky river beds; fast pistes on the plains; dunes around Erg Chebbi with rocks and sand; digging vehicles out of dunes; and the challenges of special stages, navigation and secret checkpoints.

In eight intense days of competition covering over 1,200 miles of North Africa's sand dunes, the Rallye highlighted serious technical issues as well as many smaller teething problems. In the arid Moroccan desert, the team experienced everything from near-exhaustion to punctures caused by camel grass, from brake failure to unbelievable flips in the Wildcats. Thankfully everyone came back in one piece and with a lot more information on board, including the knowledge that there are different types of sand depending on the wind direction.

⬆ Tom Neathway and Dave Marsh
tackle the dunes of the Erg Chebbi

⬇ Crews line up for the
'Wacky Races' style start

Teething problems

Before the two rally teams, two support teams and one supervision team even set foot on the sand or had a chance to put their keys in the ignition, problems arose on the journey over. The event began poorly for Ben Gott and Tony Harris as their car, the RatCat, cut out as it was boarding the ferry from Almeria to Nador. A broken fuel pump was found to be the culprit and Dave Reeve and his mechanic crew were soon on the case fixing it. Everyone eventually arrived safely and geared up for the solid week of hard work ahead.

Tony and Ben had no problems on the first day, apart from the trip computer failing to work when they went over 65mph, and they made it safely through to the service area at Missor ready to prepare for day two. But Dave Marsh and Tom Neathway in the Orange Plant Wildcat weren't so lucky. The relaxed ferry crossing the pair had enjoyed didn't set the tone for the rest of the day. Dave lost the brakes while on the navigational section and on investigating that problem they realised the wheel bearing had failed – and only the brake disc was holding the wheel on to the car! Thankfully a Portuguese Wildcat team were able to come to their aid, as the R2R service crew were an hour away. They helped change the bearing, allowing Dave and Tom to continue an action-packed day.

'We had a bit of a fright on the ferry and also lost the trip computer whenever we went over 65mph, which was most of the time, but we really enjoyed the first day of the event.'

Ben Gott, driver

Weather woes

The Moroccan climate was fickle. The team had to contend with sandstorms, dense fog and searing sunlight, but it was probably the perfect way to prepare for the challenges that lay ahead on the Dakar.

At times, the elements made their presence felt, resulting in engines lacking the power to pull the lads out of the deep sand and forcing them to retire from a stage. The mechanics struggled to work on the engines in the middle of a sandstorm and then one spectacular roll, end-over-end, caused the team's eventual withdrawal from the stage due to the engine mount failing. Frustrations like these tested the lads but were all good learning experiences. Despite the vast amount of information each member had to absorb, and increasing fatigue, their sense of humour and patience never faltered.

'I'm pleased with the way the team dealt with the complications,' commented team manager 'Pav' Taylor. 'We had the right people in the right place at the right time. The team is working very well together and we knew we had a huge amount to learn and we're doing just that – moving forward all the time.'

A good egg

Early in the week, Phillip Gillespie, aka 'Barney', showed the team his versatile personality when he had to change roles unexpectedly. Within two hours of arriving he was asked to stand in as a co-driver for a fellow competitor, due to illness. Barney relinquished his mechanic's job, albeit just for that week, and gladly jumped at the chance to enjoy driving with a Dakar veteran.

'My feet had hardly touched the ground before I was strapped into the co-driver's seat and being given my instructions,' he said gleefully. 'Our car won one of the special stages and also finished runner-up in another so I was thrilled. It was a great day, made better by the fact it was my first ever rally!'

↑ Top: Tony Harris, Tom Neathway and 'Barney' Gillespie take a break after a stage. Above: Ben getting used to sand ladders

← Dave Marsh gets to work on a broken wheel bearing

'It's not all about speed — sometimes you really need to slow down, check and carry on.'

Tony Harris, driver

Yellow jaws

The enormous sand dunes were attacked with respect after they took both teams by surprise in the early stages. The two cars suffered at the hands of their 'yellow jaws' but were in no way disheartened. Barney was quick to announce that his was the only car which didn't roll during the rally – but as the rest of the team pointed out, he'd had the most rest and had even managed a lie in!

In the final special stage, Dave and Tom gave the team a last-minute scare when their car rolled in treacherous cross-ruts, but they arrived at the finish with no further problems. As Dave said later: 'The dunes caught us out early on. We came over a crest and I felt the sand start to give way. I turned the car to drive away but the whole thing went sideways and dug itself in. We were lucky not to go over but we were well and truly stuck. Luckily there was a local tribesman passing and he helped us out.'

A knife-edged sand dune was to blame for the unlucky roll experienced by Tony's and Ben's car after they'd attacked it with a little too much power.

'Our two rolls were expensive mistakes to make and can't happen again,' said Tony, 'but we made sure we didn't push the cars to full speed as we need to drive to survive – it's a long game.'

Winners!

After tireless hours spent driving, navigating and fixing endless parts under the light of the moon, the teams achieved an extraordinary result on their international rally debut. Both R2R Wildcats finished the eight-day event and, in the process, also claimed a stage win for each competing member of the team.

Dave and Tom clearly demonstrated their grasp of the Orange Plant Wildcat and their understanding of the terrain by claiming the team's first rally stage win on the final day of the action. They also finished in 10th place overall – not bad at all for amateur drivers – and proved their sceptics wrong. Many of the professional outfits competing on the Tuareg had begun by underestimating the team's capability, but the majority were very supportive and were soon urging the lads on at every stage.

→ The manic finale
of the Tuareg Rallye

⤓ The team
celebrate their
success; both
Wildcats finished,
10th and 25th

'I'm really happy with how the event has gone and it has been a huge learning curve,' Tom said. 'Dave and I worked really well together and also learned that, sometimes, we need to rein things back a little.'

The RatCat team – Ben and Tony – shared the driving and navigational duties. Although they had their fair share of difficulties, they notched up the third of the team's fastest times, finishing 25th when they crossed the line. As Ben said, 'It's a brilliant team and a brilliant effort by everyone. We got both cars home, and we couldn't have taken anything more away from the event.'

The finish was mind-blowing. Champagne flowed – it would have given the Formula 1 boys a run for their millions – with over a thousand people waiting at the line, clapping and cheering all the drivers. Team manager 'Pav' Taylor summed up the team's feelings. 'To see the two cars sitting under the banner in a professional race made me feel so proud of all the guys. It's hard to explain to the public what these injured men have gone through just to be strapped into their seats – and no, they don't want pity, they're just keen to show the world that life does go on and dreams can be realised.'

Checklist for next time...

Many of us can relate to the summer holiday niggles caused by sand getting stuck in our shoes, but for Tony Harris the conditions on the rally proved a little more serious. Due to the heat and dehydration setting in, he became aware that his prosthetic leg started to feel different. 'One thing I did learn was how my leg behaves. As the day wears on the fitting loosens up, so I need to carry an additional sock to make sure it keeps a good, tight fit for later in the day and to avoid sores,' he explained. One more thing to add to the checklist for the Dakar...

Sleep is vital, and the lack of it could cause problems, so the guys needed to get lots in before the big event in January. The team were all exhausted before the Tuareg week even started, due to taking an overnight ferry and driving around 600 miles just to reach the start – all with only three hours' sleep.

'It was a real eye-opener for everyone – a big step up from just doing a weekend rally to eight full-on days of driving,' explained Pav, sporting only small bags under his eyes. 'There were also a lot of repairs needed on the cars after each day of racing so that limited the amount of rest for all of us. It was definitely worth it, though, when we reached the finish and had two cars under the banner.'

It may sound obvious, but the USN nutritional drinks really made a difference to the lads. Racing under the midday sun and then working on the cars in the evening, there was never time to rustle up a snack. A packed lunch would have been squashed within minutes out on the dunes, while Dave's favourite cheese and pickle sandwich would have disappeared in three gulps! The guys had to make do with sugary drinks, cleverly disguised as something to do with fruits of the forest or tropical orange.

Pav, the team manager, summed it all up. 'It has been an incredible experience for us all. The planning, preparation and not least the time involved that all the team members have given up – I can't thank them enough. Here's to the next one, boys!'

'It has been an incredible experience for us all. The planning, preparation and not least the time involved that all the team members have given up – I can't thank them enough. Here's to the next one, boys!'

**Andrew 'Pav' Taylor,
Team Manager**

← The RatCat stops for a
roll around in the desert

↑ A dusty Tony Harris
reflects on the experience

'It's all a bit surreal. 'We've had so much attention. Spectators want our autographs and just about every news agency in the world wants to talk to us. It's nuts and so much bigger than we ever thought it would be!'

Corporal Tom Neathway

RACE2RECOVERY
TO SOUTH AMERICA

The Dakar Rally is often described as the toughest race in the world – a bold statement by anyone's standards. Drivers from all over the world and from many different backgrounds enter the event each year and try to conquer the dunes, but only some 40% succeed in crossing the finishing line. Some of the best long-distance rally drivers crash out on day one, only highlighting to those amateur competitors like our Race2Recovery team that no matter how much knowledge or experience teams have, this gruelling challenge can present some nasty surprises. What matters is the here and now, taking every day and stage as it comes… so what were the chances of our Race2Recovery cars making it?

The Dakar Rally (or simply 'the Dakar', formerly known as 'the Paris–Dakar') is a supreme example of human sporting endeavour, a 15-day challenge which takes drivers and their support teams across some 5,500 miles (8,500km) of the world's most stunning – and unforgiving – deserts. Organised by the Amaury Sport Organisation (ASO), it's not just a race but an orienteering challenge too, where the teamwork of the crew is paramount if success is to be achieved. From the drivers and navigators to the mechanics, technical staff and team managers, each crew member must play their part to perfection.

The Dakar's special stages (SS) can be murderous in length. The toughest stages are a furious 250 miles (400km) of extreme off-road racing on courses where vehicles are driven at their absolute limit, jarring the body for up to 12 hours a day in a hot, noisy cabin.

As well as the SS each day, there are often liaison (or link) stages as it isn't always possible – for logistical, safety and security reasons – to begin and end an SS at the overnight bivouac sites. In these cases, race vehicles must proceed from the bivouac site to the SS start point, complete the SS, then proceed from the SS finish point to the next bivouac. After the rigours of an SS, driving the liaison stage to that night's bivouac can often be mind-numbing because of fatigue and also speed restriction, as the Dakar organising committee requires liaison stages to be completed at an average speed no higher than 100kph (62mph).

Teamwork

Many rally drivers say that the relationship with the navigator/co-driver is like a marriage. It's hard to remain amicable all the time when you live with someone, so imagine spending up to 18 hours a day in a confined space, facing constant danger while suffering from a distinct lack of sleep and still having to be civil to each other! Quin Evans, a professional navigator and R2R's principal and navigational instructor, knows only too well how the partnership between driver and navigator can make or break a race, and he sums it up perfectly.

'A good navigator is incredible – I'll let you know when I have finally achieved "incredible"!' Quin joked before he set off for South America.

⬇ **Just some of the many and varied vehicles and terrains of the Dakar Rally**

A navigator has to draw on all his senses. This may sound strange, but consider that he has to do everything from reading the road book and directing the driver for route selection, to listening to the engine for any problems and feeling if the vehicle is struggling as the sand gets softer, to using smell to alert him if the car is suffering with a slipping clutch.

'In general terms, you want a happy feeling that everything is coming together,' Quin explained. 'Until you hit the next waypoint, which could be 200km away, you're constantly checking that everything is "right" to the best of your ability. Even a huge danger like a cliff can be a great relief because, if it matches your road book, you know you're not too far off course.'

The challenges facing a

⬆ **Quin Evans discusses the next day's plan with team manager 'Pav' Taylor**

⬇ **Bride and Joy – the driver/navigator relationship is much like a marriage**

navigator on the Dakar are many and varied, as Quin highlights. 'Imagine racing from London to Bordeaux in one day without a single road, and the track you're using isn't "safe". There could be a hole big enough to swallow the vehicle at any point yet you're trying to push speeds of 100mph. Even though your road book may show the "cautions" observed by the recce crew, these may have changed with the weather or you may even be on one of the numerous parallel tracks just a few metres away from where you should be. There may be a danger that isn't marked and this is a factor in many accidents on the Dakar – the road book

THE NAVIGATOR'S EQUIPMENT

For those who don't have petrol or oil running through their veins, here are five short definitions of the tools used by navigators.

Road book In theory a turn-by-turn instruction manual of where to go, where to turn, the obstacles/dangers to avoid or be aware of, and at what distances to expect each instruction.

GPS This is used more often these days to highlight mistakes. GPS has a 'compass', telling drivers the direction they are heading, and this is used in conjunction with the road book; but it doesn't tell them where they are or where they should be going, only when they have 'arrived' at a specific point.

Trip computer The trip computer is a simple device that tells the crew how far the car has travelled – regardless of the direction – with the facility to record not only an overall distance but also a second 'intermediate' distance that can be reset between each instruction in the road book. Inaccuracies can soon creep in once the vehicle enters the sand, as episodes of wheel-spinning may suggest that the car has travelled further than it actually has.

Route topography This is a wonderful little guide, often referred to as the 'bible'. It shows what to expect on each stage (for example, when in the stage to expect dunes, rocks, mountains, rivers, etc) and the timings for stages. It's often more of a 'nice' addition than an essential item.

Route distances and timings This information gives specific timings that must be adhered to and indicates what penalties will be incurred for not reaching particular points at specified times. A navigator won't refer to information on route distances and timings unless something goes wrong and it becomes necessary to work out what the options are.

THE NAVIGATOR'S JOB

What happens once both driver and navigator are in the car and waiting to start that day's stage? There are 15 crucial steps that the navigator must take throughout the day to ensure the car finishes the stage successfully – and they leave no time at all to admire the stunning scenery or take photos.

1 Follow the road book and guide the driver through the stage by using hand signals and markers that are easy to spot, so the driver understands more readily.

2 Keep resetting the trip at each point where the road book allows clear confirmation.

3 Inform the driver of what is coming up in terms of terrain.

4 Keep the driver informed of the location of other vehicles, in as matter of fact a way as possible.

5 Respond to any Sentinel alerts (overtaking or stranded vehicles).

6 Check temperatures and levels and react accordingly.

7 Deflate tyres before dunes to maintain traction and re-inflate afterwards to reduce the risk of punctures.

8 Regularly feed the driver and yourself and ensure both of you stay hydrated.

9 Confirm you have hit each waypoint, choosing the best route to each, and don't follow a straight line as you are likely to go straight into a sand bowl.

10 Observe other vehicles – where did they get stuck or hit rough ground? Do not follow instructions from spectators.

11 Keep checking the road book to make sure you are on the right track.

12 Observe speed zones and do not race in them.

13 Have the timecard ready for CPs (checkpoints), holding it through the window to be stamped.

14 Make notes of any damage or other issues and any time lost due to changing tyres or helping others.

15 Ensure you go through each CP and finish from the correct direction, regardless of which direction you may have approached it from initially.

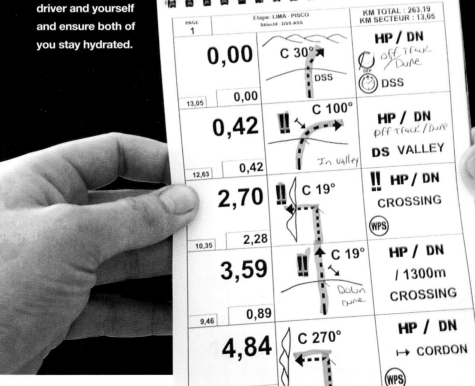

shows a fast track but, in fact, you're on a parallel track approaching a hole that needs to be taken at 10mph.'

There's no doubt that the navigator is under intense pressure. There's a lot more to deal with than just giving instructions to the driver and 'managing' him, because as soon as things start to go wrong the navigator's workload increases hugely.

During the Dakar, it was intended that the four Wildcats would run in two pairs, providing mutual support to each other across the course, with the T4 Renault Kerax following the same piste and offering an 'AA'-type service function with essential but limited mechanical and spares support. The 8x8s, which provided the team's service areas, and the Land Rovers, which transported the mechanics and team management, would follow on a separate liaison route.

A conventional day would see racers spending up to 12 hours or more in their Wildcats and the T4 Kerax race truck, covering anywhere between 400–800km (250–500 miles), largely off-road. The 17-strong 'Assistance Team' – comprising logistics experts, mechanics and team management – would follow a slightly different route, but it often isn't any less arduous. Most of the mechanics only sleep for a couple of hours each night, sometimes in small, claustrophobic pop-up tents or, if the cars are late into the bivouac, then space blankets under the stars may just have to do.

To drive for more than 5,000 miles across some of the most inhospitable terrain in South America in 15 days at speeds of up to 100mph is no mean feat, and

with only one rest day the competitors need to go the distance before they can recharge.

Peru is where it all kicked off in 2013, and this was also the first time the Dakar had started in the middle of desert. There would be no room for improvisation, with the vehicles facing the largest chains of dunes crossed on the continent since 2009. Adapting to different types of driving would be crucial as the rally reached Argentina because, although the sand there is less dense, the event's visit to Gaucho country would finish with a major test in which only genuine desert-driving experts would feel at ease. Finally the competitors would face Chile and the Atacama Desert, with stages through dunes continuing right up to the day before the finish in Santiago, with the competitors having to face extreme challenges right up to the very end of the event.

⬆ **Mark Cullum gives the T4 a boost in the dunes**

⬇ **The Orange Plant and RatCat running as a pair**

Departure from the UK

In late November 2012, the team were ready to ship the vehicles and the massive amounts of logistical stores that would be needed in South America.

During the build-up 'Pav' Taylor, John Winskill and Matt O'Hare sat down and reviewed the final version of the race entry list. It transpired that Race2Recovery were the only team in the 2013 Dakar to be entering five race vehicles in the competition. Even the Monster Energy factory BMW Mini team, the all-out favourites, were only entering three vehicles, while the multi-million-dollar Qatar/Red Bull team led by Carlos Sainz and Nasser Al-Attiyah were fielding just two buggies! Undaunted by this revelation the R2R convoy, resplendent in its white livery, departed their headquarters in Alton, Hampshire on a suitably dramatic and very rainy night and headed to Portsmouth for the ferry to Caen on the first leg to reach South America.

The Lazer Lights mounted to each front bumper gave the Wildcats the appearance of extra-terrestrial star fighters, perhaps better suited to a Hollywood movie than a desert race! The lights, however, couldn't hide the grins of their elated drivers – Matt in his lovable but temperamental Joy; Ben in his steed, known by all as the RatCat; Tony in the newest vehicle of the fleet, the I.R.D. ('International Rally Driver'); and Justin in the late Gordon Chapman's Wildcat, now emblazoned with the name of Gordon's beloved company, Orange Plant.

Flying line-astern and in close formation with the Wildcats was the team's T4 Renault Kerax race truck, with its 700hp fully tuned race motor on full song. For the journey to France, the Kerax was driven by its race co-driver, Chris Ratter, as the truck's race driver, Mark Cullum, had work commitments. Following the howling procession of race vehicles were the assistance team, in a mixture of 4x4 and 8x8 vehicles. First were the two Land Rover-supplied Discovery 4x4s in very suitable matching British Racing Green colours, for the team management and mechanics. Just about keeping up was the massively practical silver Defender 130, specifically selected for its capacity to move spares and tyres around the bivouac sites. Glued to the tail lights of the Defender, and announcing the big boys' arrival, were the monstrous 8x8 support trucks – the DAF Drops (aka 'the Duff') and the MAN Kat T5. These behemoths, which carried the majority of the team's equipment, stores and mechanical spares in their dismountable box body rear sections, were driven to France by Chris Astles and Martyn Williams, the men who would drive them on the Dakar itself. Two more Discovery 4x4s completed the convoy, containing the Gaucho film crew who would accompany the team throughout the adventure, seeking to capture every moment for posterity.

⬇ The team at Heathrow, bright and very early

NO JOY IN LE HAVRE

The first leg of the journey to South America was to travel to Le Havre, France, where the R2R convoy would be loaded on the *CSAV Rio Imperial* for the sea voyage to Lima, Peru, via the Panama Canal.

Even before they left home soil, however, problems quickly presented themselves and the mechanics were put to work sooner than they had anticipated! Ironically, it was Joy, driven by Matt O'Hare, that made life difficult from the word go…

'I'd asked Matt to call me to let me know how it was going,' said 'Barney' Gillespie, Joy's navigator. 'When he told me Joy had broken down and was overheating, I thought, "Oh great, here we go, we're taking an overheating car to South America at the hottest time of the year – what chance have we got?". But we would have five days in Lima before the race started so we hoped the mechanics would be able to sort it out…"

On arrival in Caen the convoy left for Le Havre but after about 30km Joy decided to blow a plastic plug out of the header tank of her cooling system and dump most of the water. Chris Ratter, following in the T4 Kerax, dutifully stopped.

'We replaced the plug with a bolt,' said Chris, 'and then refilled the system with coolant. As the radiator is in the back of the Wildcat and the engine is in the front, removing all the air from the system is a challenge at the best of times – let alone on the hard shoulder of a French motorway in pouring rain!'

Unfortunately some air remained in the system so, although all seemed sorted, Joy only travelled another 7km before she started boiling again. This time reinforcements were called up in the form of Sean Whatley, who was towing a trailer carrying a spare vehicle to take the convoy drivers back to the UK; Joy was put on the trailer instead and resumed her journey. When they finally reached Le Havre, the air was bled out of the cooling system only for another problem to occur – the selector shaft seal on the gearbox blew out and dumped most of the gearbox oil. Time for a deep breath…

Eventually, with a replacement seal fitted and the gearbox replenished with oil, they were able to set off into scrutineering, where Joy sailed through with flying colours, to huge sighs of relief all round.

⬆ The Wildcats prepare for their long sea voyage to South America on the 46,800-tonne *CSAV Rio Imperial*

While the Race2Recovery vehicles travelled by sea from Le Havre to Lima, team personnel, of course, flew to Peru. For all the Brits this meant an early-morning start at Heathrow on New Year's Eve for a connecting flight to Madrid and from there to Lima. Cathy Derousseaux joined the guys in Madrid, while US Marines Mark Zambon and Tim Read flew direct from their home country. With the time difference, the team arrived in Lima in time for a celebratory dinner that same evening, though most of them, somewhat unusually, were too tired to see in the New Year!

Arrival in South America

The heat and humidity of Peru on New Year's Eve was a world away from friends, family and Auld Lang Syne. The focus now for the team, based at the official rally headquarters on the coast at Lima, was the Dakar itself: would they cope with the vast distances and dangers, and could they reach the finish?

⬇ The fleet line up after unloading at Port Callao, Lima

New Year's Day saw drivers and co-drivers go to Port Callao to be reunited with their vehicles, which had been offloaded from the *CSAV Rio Imperial* before Christmas by locally employed civilian staff. Here the team were able to carry out some minor mechanical work, including topping up the oils on car 445, Joy, who refused to start; not a particularly positive sign for their first day in South America. En masse, the team then moved on under police escort and established themselves in the assistance park on the beach in Miraflores. This was the ideal time and location for last-minute checks and adjustments, including verifying the relevant spares that would be carried on the race-support T4 truck and vital work on the Orange Plant Wildcat's steering. This was also a good opportunity to meet up with other teams and get some valuable pre-race advice.

Nestling below stark sea cliffs and stretching for several kilometres, the beach at Miraflores would be the team's forward operating base until the Dakar started on 5 January. Under the direction of the team's 'bivouac meister', Marty Rae, the T5s dropped their boxes, Easy-Up sun shelters were erected, the Wildcats were raised on jacks, and the Discoveries disappeared into the city for the purchase of some last-minute provisions.

The team spent most of the day having briefings, packing personal equipment and preparing for the main focus of pre-race procedure – the dreaded scrutineering. This process is like a sausage machine, with both personnel and vehicles rigorously inspected for race readiness in all areas, from documentation to safety equipment and licences.

The team's aim at this stage was to confirm that all checks and essential servicing had been completed so as to ensure that everything met with the official requirements. The drivers and co-drivers made sure the cars were filled with all the mandatory race equipment, from sand ladders to water carriers and from rations to emergency shelters. Meanwhile, the mechanics busied themselves with last-minute servicing – 'check and test' was very much the motto through these last days. And Tony Harris even did some cleaning to make sure I.R.D. was gleaming for the off!

⬆ Jonny Koonja gives the
Orange Plant Wildcat a thorough
check before scrutineering

⬆ Lee Townsend makes
adjustments to Matt
O'Hare's steering wheel

⬇ Typically Joy had problems even
before leaving the port in Lima; but with
some fresh oil she was ready to roll

1   Four titles were up for grabs – in the bike, quad, car and truck categories.

2   In 2013 Peru hosted the start for the first time.

3   The 2013 event involved 14 days of racing.

4   The youngest competitor was 19-year-old Dutchman Robert van Pelt.

5   The oldest was 73-year-old Francisco Claudio Regunaschi.

Added difficulties

The Race2Recovery team is the first disabled team to enter the Dakar. The preparation and training for able-bodied drivers and their teams is immense, but the amount of work that went into getting the R2R guys to the start was astounding. Vehicles and crews have to be in peak condition for any team, whether able-bodied or disabled, but for the latter the cars also have to be adapted to each individual driver's needs. Nothing can be overlooked, which simply results in a need for more money, time and expertise than an able-bodied race team would require.

As an example, Tony Harris, who had a below-knee amputation of his left leg, needed a clutch that would allow him to know when he had reached the 'bite' point. This was proving impossible until the team of mechanics fitted a warning-light system to let him know when the pedal was depressed.

'We just don't know how the desert is going to affect those of us with amputations,' said Tony before the event. 'Because my prosthetic is effectively a pirate's leg, I shouldn't have too much to worry about. But Tom has electronics in his legs, involving moving parts, and we're not sure how they'll function.'

For US Marine Staff Sergeant Mark Zambon, a double above-knee amputee, and Tom Neathway, a triple amputee, attention to detail and comfort were even more important. Tom, who lost both legs above the knee as well as his left arm, took two spare sets of legs with him to withstand the extreme temperatures and shocks on the rally. His prosthetics are meant to last up to five years, but that's in 'normal' conditions

– and there's nothing normal about the Dakar! Mark, meanwhile, used his special 'car legs'; shorter than his normal prosthetics, these legs were designed to be more comfortable in the car when racing with Ben Gott, his driver. The downside was that Mark lost a few inches when upright and it took a while for the team to get used to having a 'Mini-Mark' walking around the bivouac!

Martin Colclough, Head of Physical Development at Help for Heroes, explained why the Dakar would throw things at these guys that able-bodied people wouldn't even have to think about.

'Taking themselves and their prosthetics into an incredibly harsh environment,' stated Martin before the event, 'means that, whilst prosthetics are very robust, the conditions will test their limbs to the limit because, as with all modern technology, sometimes prosthetics trade off robustness with function. The electronics contained in Tom's legs require regular battery-charging so older mechanical prosthetics may provide a more sustainable level of mobility. It's the electronics that usually fail, not the mechanical side of things. Also a mechanical prosthetic with simple shock absorbers would be simpler to fix in the field.'

Anything the team learn from operating in these extremes is fed back to the prosthetics department at Headley Court, Surrey, to aid research and development for future limbs. Soldiers who have laid their life on the line and are injured in service, resulting in amputation, benefit from a world-class prosthetic service at Headley Court along with a continued care package of full-time rehabilitation. It's often the quality of rehabilitation that provides the best rate of recovery and the optimum level to which someone can recover. In contrast, rehabilitation within the NHS can only concentrate on reaching a level of ADL – 'activities of daily living'.

The other issue to consider on the Dakar surrounded caring for their stumps. Martin continues: 'Because they lose surface area as an amputee, their core temperature remains the same as any other member of the team but their anatomy is compromised and they aren't able to lose heat as easily, therefore their physiology is compromised and the heat could affect them more than another member of the team, especially in a humid environment. Excessive sweating can lead to excess salt crystals which can act like grit on the socket, and the risk of soreness, cracking and fungal infections can increase unless they take extra care.'

← 'Mini-Mark' sporting his bespoke Dakar legs

⬇ Heat and humidity presented a real issue for Tom Neathway, swathed in carbonfibre – his body has less surface area to help him cool down

CELEBRITY STATUS
MESSAGES OF GOOD LUCK

While the team were going through final preparations in Peru, a host of celebrities and sports stars were taking to social media to wish the team well – and in doing so helping the fundraising profile of Race2Recovery. Tweets from the sports world included Paralympian David Weir MBE, Olympian Dame Kelly Holmes and England rugby captain Chris Robshaw.

'It's all a bit surreal,' said Tom Neathway. 'We've had so much attention. Spectators want our autographs and just about every news agency in the world wants to talk to us. It's nuts and so much bigger than we ever thought it would be!'

Chelsea FC – Good luck Chelsea fan Tom Neathway @race2recovery injured soldiers starting Dakar Rally 5 Jan Donate bit.ly/Rob984 #beyondinjury

Clarence House – Good luck to the injured soldiers starting Dakar Rally challenge on 5 Jan for @race2recovery - bit.ly/Rob984 #beyondinjury

Tickets for Troops – Race2Recovery set off on the Dakar Rally on Sat. Huge luck to the whole team. Amazing stuff! Donate here race2recovery.com #beyondinjury

Robbie Williams – Remember Robbie @HelpForHeroes? Pls support @Race2Recovery soldiers raising ££ for @TedworthHouse Donate bit.ly/Rob984 RT #beyondinjury

Help for Heroes - @robbiewilliams @race2recovery @tedworthhouse absolutely Robbie aren't they inspiring! We're so proud to be supporting them #beyondinjury

Charley Boorman - @charleyboorman @SimonPavey Don't forget to look out for the team of injured soldiers @Race2Recovery #Dakar2013

Ben Fogle – Good luck to @Race2Recovery who begin the Dakar Rally in Peru #beyondinjury

Pete Reed – Best wishes to the injured soldiers @race2recovery who start the Dakar Rally on Jan 5th. Amazing challenge & adventure ahead #beyondinjury

Ben Saunders – Good luck to the @race2recovery team starting the Dakar Rally on 5 jan #beyond injury

Jonathan Adams – Massive good luck @race2recovery! Injured soldiers starting Dakar Rally challenge 5 Jan. Donate at bit.ly/Rob984 RT #beyondinjury

Sam Aston - @race2recovery thanks for Rt us at corrie love your page shout be Kl lol all the best I am backing u Rt

Emme Hall - RT @jasonsharpe Here's an inspiring team of injured British servicemen competing in #Dakar race2recovery.com @race2recovery

Mel Nicholls – Best of luck @race2recovery Injured soldiers starting Dakar Rally challenge 5 Jan Please RT Donate at bit.ly/Rob984 #beyondinjury

Theo Paphitis – Best of luck to all in @race2recovery! Injured soldiers starting Dakar Rally challenge 5 Jan. Donate at bit.ly/Rob984 RT #beyondinjury

Jody Cundy MBE – All the best of luck to the guys @race2recovery! Dakar Rally challenge starts the 5th Jan at bit.ly/Rob984 RT #beyondinjury

Jake Handley – Good luck to the @Race2Recovery guys in the Dakar! It's going to be one amazing time for the guys for sure!

Ben Shephard – Evening – pls check out + follow @Race2Recovery 2morrow they start a practically impossible definitely brutal unquestionably heroic challenge

Stobart Group – Great to see @Race2Recovery team tackling Dakar and raising money for @Helpfor Heroes make sure you follow them to see how they get on!

Mercedes AMG F1 – @Race2Recovery we will! Good luck guys (in response to Race2Recovery #Dakar2013 #beyondinjury)

Scrutineering

At 11am on 3 January the team moved off to the temporary scrutineering 'hangars'. Located at the end of the beach and next to *parc fermé,* these facilities were a veritable hive of activity as the organisers' technical staff, notable for their grey 'organisation' T-shirts, crawled under, over and inside the mass of race-ready competition vehicles.

Joining the queues of weird and wonderful multi-coloured machines, the T4 Kerax, the Discoveries and three of the Wildcats duly arrived at their allotted slot at the required time. At the last minute, however, Tony Harris's I.R.D. refused to start, but after frantic and heroic efforts by her team of mechanics she did eventually fire up. Fearful of incurring significant financial penalties by missing their time slot, Tony leapt aboard and roared down the access road with his co-pilot Cathy Derousseaux literally hanging on to the outside of the car – she hadn't had time to get properly into her seat before Tony dropped the clutch and headed off! Thanks to a kind Peruvian policeman, who held up an enormous line of traffic, Tony was able to screech a U-turn into the entrance gate where John Winskill was waiting to hand him his essential paperwork and point him in the right direction for the scrutineering lane. They'd made it and didn't incur any penalty – beyond a Gallic shrug from a sweating French official!

'This was a stressful time for all of us,' said John, the team's logistic support co-ordinator and communications manager. 'We had spent many, many weeks studying endless FIA regulations to ensure we were entirely compliant with the rules as laid down by the ASO, but you never really know if you've got it right until they stamp your card and wave you through.'

The feeling of relief in the team was palpable, but success at this important stage was no mere formality. Some competitors' vehicles were actually excluded from the race for rule-book infringements, shattering their crews' dreams of Dakar glory. It was a testimony to the preparations that the team had conducted in the UK, and to Chris Ratter's almost encyclopaedic knowledge of the rule book, that all the team's vehicles were declared compliant. Very few alterations were needed, save for a quick drill of Joy's engine block by Jonny Koonja, to facilitate the ASO fixing a sealing wire to prevent unlawful 'adjustments' to her engine during the event.

Amid the mêlée of scrutineering and the heat and the dust of the day, the team's notoriety had clearly preceded them. As R2R drivers, mechanics and assistance crews all fought to ensure their vehicles progressed through the line of ASO checks,

they were literally mobbed by adoring Dakar fans. The team's collection of flyers practically became a currency with the delightful, enthusiastic and very energetic Peruvian fans, being almost ripped from the team members' grasp such was the ardour

↑ **The four Wildcats lined up for scrutineering**

← **The team are put through their paces – scenes from scrutineering**

↑ Jonny Koonja, Rick Nixon and Dave Reeve
give the Orange Plant Wildcat some TLC

↓ Tim Hare treats the navigators
to lunch and admires their legs

and adulation being shown. Posters, national flags, T-shirts, hats and even babies were thrust upon the R2R guys to have a signature scrawled across them. The team's second-youngest member, 23-year-old Martyn Williams, was quite shocked when a very well-endowed Venezuelan lady opened her blouse and requested he autograph her ample cleavage!

It wasn't all camera flashes and autographs, though. With the cars finally in the *parc fermé* compound and ready for the off, the team had to wash clothes, gather their thoughts and savour the comfort of a real bed. This is what Tim Hare reported on his blog: 'We treated ourselves to a few cheeky beers as the laptops, race suits and spanners were packed away until race day. Our beds were soon calling, as was the need to get as much rest as possible – we don't know when we'll get another proper night's sleep, probably in over a fortnight!'.

The date of 5 January 2013 had been etched in the team's minds since that first day at Headley Court when Tom and Tony started their research. Now it was finally upon them...

← **Success! Tony Harris gives the thumbs up on passing scrutineering**

⬇ **The cars enter** *parc fermé* **prior to race day**

RACE2RECOVERY
DAKAR RALLY

STAGE 1 — **Saturday 5th January:** Lima – Pisco — **120**
Road sections: **250km** • Special stage: **13km**

STAGE 2 — **Sunday 6th January:** Pisco – Pisco — **126**
Road sections: **85km** • Special stage: **242km**

STAGE 3 — **Monday 7th January:** Pisco – Nazca — **130**
Road sections: **100km** • Special stage: **243km**

STAGE 4 — **Tuesday 8th January:** Nazca – Arequipa — **136**
Road sections: **429km** • Special stage: **288km**

STAGE 5 — **Wednesday 9th January:** Arequipa – Arica — **140**
Road sections: **337km** • Special stage: **172km**

STAGE 6 — **Thursday 10th January:** Arica – Calama — **144**
Road sections: **313km** • Special stage: **454km**

STAGE 7 — **Friday 11th January:** Calama – Salta — **150**
Road sections: **534km** • Special stage: **220km**

STAGE 8 — **Saturday 12th January:** Salta – San Miguel de Tucumán — **152**
Road sections: **379km** • Special stage: **470km**

STAGE 9 — **Monday 14th January:** San Miguel de Tucumán – Córdoba — **160**
Road sections: **259km** • Special stage: **593km**

STAGE 10 — **Tuesday 15th January:** Córdoba – La Rioja — **164**
Road sections: **279km** • Special stage: **353km**

STAGE 11 — **Wednesday 16th January:** La Rioja – Fiambalá — **168**
Road sections: **262km** • Special stage: **219km**

STAGE 12 — **Thursday 17th January:** Fiambalá – Copiapó — **170**
Road sections: **396km** • Special stage: **319km**

STAGE 13 — **Friday 18th January:** Copiapó – La Serena — **174**
Road sections: **294km** • Special stage: **441km**

STAGE 14 — **Saturday 19th January:** La Serena – Santiago — **176**
Road sections: **502km** • Special stage: **128km**

STAGE 1 • 5 JANUARY 2013
LIMA TO PISCO

The fact that teamwork is the key to success on an event like the Dakar Rally was highlighted on the very first day.

That morning saw the four Wildcats and the T4 Kerax race truck depart *parc fermé* and head for the official start ramp in front of huge crowds. After leaving the ramp at their allotted time slots, they would drive the 252km liaison route southwards on main roads before turning into the desert for the first special stage and the inevitable sand dunes. From previous experience of Dakar starts, the team principal, Quin Evans knew that the city would rapidly become gridlocked as hundreds of thousands of excited spectators mobbed the streets in anticipation of the pageant that was a Dakar start, so he took the decision to despatch a small advance party drawn from the assistance team to leave before first light.

This advance party comprised three vehicles. John Winskill, the team's logistics manager and driver of the Land Rover Defender 130, took with him mechanics Jonny Koonja, Dave Reeve and Tim Read. The heavy lifters of the advance party would come from the big T5 assistance trucks: the DAF driven by Chris Astles with mechanic Sean Whatley alongside him and the MAN Kat driven by Martyn Williams with mechanics Rick Nixon and Gareth Paterson on board. Their task was to beat the traffic chaos and head directly to the first bivouac near Pisco, in order to give the assistance team enough time to prepare the service bays for the cars, given that this was their first 'real' bivouac. As the first day's stage was a mere 13km, it was expected that the cars would be arriving by mid-afternoon.

⬇ The luxury tented encampment that would be home for the next fortnight

← Tony Harris and Cathy Derousseaux leave the podium to begin their Dakar adventure

↓ Justin Birchall and Tom Neathway take a leap into the unknown

← Matt O'Hare adjusting the HANS (Head and Neck Support) device on Barney's helmet

→ The vehicles wait in *parc fermé* for their turn on the start podium

⬇ Ben Gott and Mark Zambon pass the crowds. It was estimated that between 500,000 and 1,000,000 people lined the route through Lima

'It has been a long, long day but everyone has been fantastic and it shows the spirit of the Dakar that we were helped by another team.'

Tony Harris

Quin briefed the advance party in the dark foyer of their hotel before departure at 4.00am. As the hotel car park was too small for the monster T5 trucks, they had been parked down on the beach at the scrutineering area, near the Wildcats and the T4 Kerax, and therefore the five-strong T5 crew dumped their coloured Ortleib expedition bags in the boots of two pre-booked taxis. The little convoy, the Defender and two taxis, headed through dark, silent streets down to the beach front to collect the two T5 trucks.

The drive south down the Pan-American highway was uneventful despite the blazing summer heat, and after four and a half hours the advance party saw telltale signs of activity, with large numbers of military and police vehicles as well as numerous civilian cars pulled over. Squinting through the heat haze, the R2R guys saw the flutter of the Dakar sponsor flags and a dust cloud rising from a large group of vehicles and trucks heading uphill, off the road and into the hinterland. The first bivouac had been reached.

It soon transpired that the crew's early departure hadn't been mirrored by the majority of the race teams and that they were almost the first to arrive. This proved excellent news, as the pick of the bivouac site was theirs for the taking. The early starts were proving quite a mission already for stores manager Gareth, who fell

→ Sean Whatley
getting to work
on the RatCat

↓ Tony Harris
identifies the front
differential problem
on the I.R.D. Wildcat

asleep whilst changing his socks one morning and had to be woken by Chris Bayliss!

But issues arose for the team on this very first day. The racing pairs, who had been able to enjoy breakfast at the hotel before leaving to collect their cars from *parc fermé*, had been hoping for a smooth run on the 13km first stage, but Lady Luck wasn't smiling on them. I.R.D., crewed by Tony Harris and Cathy Derousseaux, developed a problem with its front differential, forcing the support team into action before Tony had even put the accelerator down in anger. The crew worked their magic and removed a transmission shaft, allowing the car to start in two-wheel drive.

The first special stage was designed as a sort of appetiser, to allow the crews to get a taste of the challenges to come and try to ease them in, but in the desert there's no such thing as an 'easy' stage. Four or five kilometres in and I.R.D. was in trouble again; Tony telephoned the team to report a problem with the rear of the car but had to wait, stranded in the desert, because he was reliant on the team's race and support truck, the T4 Renault Kerax, which hadn't yet entered the stage and wouldn't do so for two more hours. The Kerax was filled with an array of spares to fix the cars on the special stages and even had the equipment to tow them to the end of a stage if the need arose, which it did.

When they arrived the Kerax crew – Mark Cullum, Charles Sincock and Chris Ratter – decided the only option was to tow I.R.D. back to the bivouac for repair as the rear differential needed to be replaced. However, this wasn't without its own problems: despite taking advice from locals on the best way to navigate back, the T4, laden with spares and with the additional weight of Tony and Cathy's Wildcat on the back, struggled to get out of a sand bowl and got stuck. So with I.R.D. still attached, the support team enlisted the help of some more locals to unhook and set up sand ladders to extract the T4 – all 14 tonnes of it complete with load. Unfortunately, there was

also a problem – unknown to the crew at this time – with the truck's tyre-inflation system showing false pressure readings, and this led to the pressure of the front right tyre being dropped too low and unseating it...

It took four hours to extract the T4 and it was an epic job. Sand had to be excavated from underneath it to create room for jacking it up and re-seating the tyre, only for the sand to keep flowing back into the hole. However, in true Dakar spirit, assistance came from the French Team Boucou whose trucks stopped to help pull the Race2Recovery personnel out in order to finally get to the bivouac.

It wasn't the best start for Tony and Cathy, but it made clear to everyone the gruelling nature of what they had undertaken and how the dunes really can throw up major problems at any time, no matter how short or long the stage.

'We knew the Dakar was going to be tough and today we learnt just how tough,' said Tony when they reached the bivouac and had a chance to rest at last. 'It has been a long, long day but everyone has been fantastic and it shows the spirit of the Dakar that we were helped by another team. Tomorrow is another day and the main thing is that we're still in this amazing event. There's a reason they call this the world's toughest rally...'

STAGE 1
LIMA TO PISCO

Road sections	250km
Special stage	13km
Total	263km

Car	Time	Variation	
Orange Plant	11m 02s	3m 22s	84th
RatCat	14m 57s	7m 17s	131st
Joy	16m 44s	9m 04s	133rd
I.R.D.	3h 45m	3h 37m 20s	151st

Truck	Time	Variation	
T4	3h 45m	3h 36m 14s	75th

Joy tackles the liaison stage in Pisco

STAGE 2 · 6 JANUARY 2013
PISCO TO PISCO

Again it was Tony Harris and Cathy Derousseaux who stole the attention on the second day, but unfortunately again not for the right reasons. More technical problems on the day's special stage meant the race truck was called upon again to look after I.R.D., with the expertise of the Kerax crew again tested.

Thankfully the Wildcat was repaired successfully and the duo was able to drive on into the night through some of the most taxing dunes the rally would encounter. They made it safely to the bivouac, but concerns were quickly raised that they'd missed some of the waypoints on the stage. The team had no choice but to consult the rally organisers and although they were fined, with some significant time penalties, they were given the green light to continue the following day.

'The last 48 hours have been an emotional rollercoaster,' said Tony. 'It hasn't been the start we wanted, but we've both snatched some sleep and

⬆ Matt O'Hare keeps cool – unlike his steed

⬇ The T4 support crew come to the aid of Tony and Cathy (again) for electrical problems

we're off to the start line. We still have all four cars and we're learning all the time.'

Meanwhile the Kerax was going on a diet to enable it to negotiate the incredible sand seas with minimum weight whilst keeping appropriate momentum.

'The key is to reduce pressure generated across the tyre footprint,' Mark Cullum explained. 'You're far more able to negotiate sand dunes and ascend soft terrain with lower weight across the wheels whilst being able to apply high engine torque to maintain rolling effort on the tyres to prevent the engine literally running out of puff.'

The T4 also came to the assistance of other teams on stage including stopping to right the Toyota of Luis Antonio Mendoza after it rolled down a 30m dune.

Joy, the Wildcat crewed by Barney Gillespie and Matt O'Hare, enjoyed another quiet day without much excitement, but when Ben Gott and US Marine Mark Zambon in the RatCat and Justin Birchall and Tom Neathway in the Orange Plant arrived back well ahead of Joy, rumours set in. Never listen to rumours – they're

⬆ **Joy on a twilight run**

⬇ **Race2Recovery support crew assisting Argentine Luis Antonio Mendoza's Toyota**

← All hands come together to work on Joy's overheating problems

⬇ The bivouac at night

'For Matt and Barney to navigate back through the night was an awesome achievement.'

Quin Evans, Team Principal

nearly always incorrect – and that was the case when whispers circulated that Joy was in trouble on the stage and wasn't going to make it back in time. But at 9.20pm, 40 minutes before the cut-off point, she rolled into the camp with Matt and Barney beaming from ear to ear – another day ticked off.

'She kept overheating every 30km or so, so we had to stop, take a break and let her cool down,' said Barney after safely returning to camp. 'Matt did a brilliant job and we're still here. I've never seen dunes like that and we were navigating through them in the dark. This is everything I thought the Dakar would be.'

Both Matt and Barney had to adopt some drastic ways of staying awake as so much of their Dakar journey would be done at night – techniques included hitting themselves round the face, reminiscent of a scene from the film *Dumb and Dumber*!

Team Principal and navigation expert, Quin Evans, said from the camp: 'These early days were among the most challenging ever seen on the Dakar, with extremely difficult dune sections to contend with that caused a headache for even the most experienced competitors. All our crews have done a great job – for Matt and Barney to navigate back through the night was an awesome achievement.'

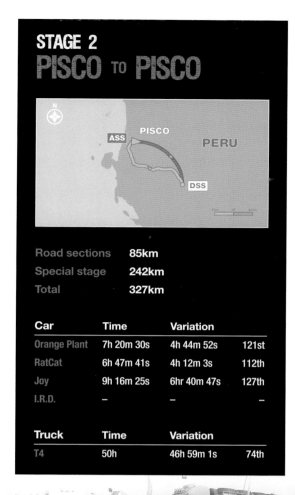

STAGE 2
PISCO TO PISCO

Road sections	85km
Special stage	242km
Total	327km

Car	Time	Variation	
Orange Plant	7h 20m 30s	4h 44m 52s	121st
RatCat	6h 47m 41s	4h 12m 3s	112th
Joy	9h 16m 25s	6hr 40m 47s	127th
I.R.D.	–	–	–

Truck	Time	Variation	
T4	50h	46h 59m 1s	74th

⬇ Quin Evans (below left) rated the early days as 'among the most challenging ever seen on the Dakar'; Tim Read (below right) entertains the thought of tackling the Dakar on a motorbike!

STAGE 3 • 7 JANUARY 2013
PISCO TO NAZCA

All four cars made it to Day Three – just. But the new day once again presented fresh problems, and this time it was Ben Gott and Mark Zambon in RatCat who needed assistance from the support crew.

'At 50km we thought we were out,' said Mark. 'We had a major gearbox problem, but we worked with the Wildcat crewed by Tom and Justin and fixed it in the stage. We couldn't believe it, though, when the power steering then decided to fail and Ben had to drive through the dunes for 250km, only using the strength of his forearms – an achievement in itself. Thank goodness he spent a fair bit of time in the gym over Christmas!'

The four Wildcats joined up on the stage just before the dune fields and started picking their way through. It wasn't long before Joy started to huff and puff and run poorly, but she carried on going. All the cars then found themselves in a shallow sand bowl, a dune formation with loose, power-sapping sand at the bottom that washes away any momentum as a vehicle charges through. So with Matt and Barney losing power and struggling to keep up with the pace, the cars separated, their crews thinking it was better to get two of the Wildcats back to the mechanics in daylight rather than none at all. I.R.D. and Orange Plant did indeed make it back before nightfall, with Tony and Cathy finally having a smooth run and posting the team's best time. Matt and Barney slogged on, too, and got Joy to the end to receive a full checkover.

'It was a relief to see Matt and Barney arrive back as

Teamwork:
Orange Plant tails
RatCat, working
as a pair

there were times when none of us seemed to know where they were,' said Ben. 'Then they just appeared! We worked out what was wrong with poor Joy – fuel vaporising was the problem – and the mechanics quickly came up with various solutions.'

As Lee Townsend explained further, 'One way we tried to repair this was to go to a local DIY shop and purchase some aluminium ducting that normally would be used for a fireplace. Dave Reeve and I ran a piece from the air intake scoop so it blew on to the fuel pumps to try and cool them down.'

After the trials of the previous day's stage, these mishaps now seemed almost routine for the racing teams, but obviously the support crew could never rest easy and always had to be on the alert.

The T4 race truck, however, had more than its share of dramas on this third day. On negotiating a long, difficult dune ascent they came across an injured competitor. This turned out to be Franck Cornille of the French Boucou Assistance outfit, which provides support services to those entrants without their own back-up. Cornille had been carrying out a foot recce

when he was struck by a quad bike ridden by a local, who just rode on without stopping. His right arm, which was thought to be broken, was very painful and he had a head injury.

Charles Sincock administered basic first aid whilst Mark Cullum took the T4 to the top of the dune where

⬆ **Chris Ratter sits with injured Franck Cornille while he awaits airlift by helicopter**

> *'Ben had to drive through the dunes for 250km, only using the strength of his forearms – an achievement in itself.'*
>
> **Mark Zambon (talking about power steering failure)**

he was able to contact the ASO HQ in France by IriTrack – a safety system that allows online tracking of the racing vehicles via satellite. Fitted to all competing vehicles, IriTrack enables assistance to be summoned within minutes to any location at any time, and incidentally also allows anyone in the world to follow the race in near real-time conditions via the internet. After discussion of the situation over IriTrack, a helicopter evacuation was organised and Franck was airlifted to the next bivouac where he could receive medical attention; thankfully a field hospital with facilities equal to the best in the world was present at all the bivouacs.

From here on, the T4 Kerax crew joined up with the Boucou Assistance truck, driven by proprietor Michel Boucou, and a Saudi race truck that Boucou had assisted earlier in the day. By running the last 100km together as the light faded at the end of the

⬇ Preparing to unload the replacement 600kg transfer box. The Defender was then used to simply drag the broken box from beneath the T4 and to pull in the new box on top of the airbag used for lifting

day, they would all benefit from mutual support should any further problems arise.

As darkness descended on southern Peru, route selection became more critical and whilst leading this pack over a plateau Mark Cullum hit a rocky ledge at high speed and the front of the Kerax leaped in the air. As it did so the vehicle suddenly lost all drive: something critical had failed in the drivetrain...

T4's transfer box troubles

'We'd knackered the transfer box,' explained Chris Ratter. 'Bearing in mind that this thing is similar in size to a fridge-freezer, weighs 600kg and costs a lot, we didn't hold out much hope of sorting the problem. Our days in the Dakar were surely numbered...'

Michel Boucou tried to tow the Race2Recovery T4 Kerax but then rally officials in their sweeper truck reached the group and advised that the healthy

'I can honestly say that in my 30-year career of fixing four-wheeled vehicles that was the hardest job I've ever done.'

Chris Ratter

vehicles should continue as otherwise they would be excluded from the rally.

When the message came through to the rest of the Race2Recovery support team at that night's bivouac that the T4 had broken its transfer box, they realised straight away that the only way to fix the truck was to replace the box, something that Marty Rae, with considerable irony, judged to be 'just another problem on an already long list!'

Contrary to Chris Ratter's fears, it was possible to source a replacement transfer box, again thanks to help from the Boucou outfit, and a secondhand unit was duly purchased from them for 2,500 Euros – much less than the £10,000 that a new one would cost. Getting it to the stranded T4 crew, however, was an altogether tougher nut to crack.

'I rang Mark Cullum on the sat phone,' explained Marty, 'and he was confident that our Land Rover Defender 130 would be able to carry the weight of the replacement box. But when we were packing up the Defender, the Boucou people said we would never make it; that was like a red rag to a bull for me and I knew I had to prove them wrong. I called all the mechanics together and asked who was up for it, as I wanted a volunteer, not someone who had to be pushed into taking on the massive task ahead. Rick Nixon's hand shot up – I've only ever seen it move quicker when he puts a cigarette in his mouth!'

TRANSFER BOX

The transfer box is a major part of any all-wheel-drive (or four-wheel-drive) system and is definitely one of the most important components when it comes to making the system actually work. Without it, you have a regular two-wheel-drive vehicle on your hands – not much use in sand dunes. The transfer box connects the front and rear axles by means of drive shafts and distributes the drive to each axle.

It was 3.00am by the time Marty and Rick set off in the Defender 130 with the transfer box in the back. They reached the town nearest the T4's location at first light and eventually found the track they were looking for into the desert, even though it wasn't actually where the map indicated.

'The terrain was OK at first,' continued Marty, 'but then we hit an enormous plateau of desert – I've seen quite a few in my time but nothing like that one. We had to recce to find a way through as we had to be sensible; we couldn't afford to get stuck too – that just wasn't an option.'

With the weight of the transfer box in the back causing them increasing difficulty in the sand as they gradually closed the distance to the stricken Kerax, Marty eventually decided they could go no further. By this point, with the rescue vehicle only 2km from the T4, Marty and Mark decided that they'd leave their respective vehicles and walk to meet each other at a mid-point among the razorback dunes – hard work under the searing sun. When they connected, they decided it would be best if Marty returned to the Defender with Mark who, using all his off-road driving experience, would then drive it those last 2km.

Meanwhile the crew of the stricken T4, knowing that help was on the way, had prepared as best they could by taking out the broken transfer box during the night and cutting a hole in the truck's floor through

which the new box could be winched into place, using a makeshift crane lift made up of straps and ratchets supported by the lowering and lifting capability of one of the pressure air bags carried on the vehicle.

The feat would have been difficult in a fully kitted-out workshop, and yet these guys – against virtually all advice and opinion – managed to complete this task in the middle of the desert in deep sand, during a sandstorm, with limited equipment. As Chris stated, 'I can honestly say that in my 30-year career of fixing four-wheeled vehicles that was the hardest job I've ever done.' Fitting the replacement box, needless to say, took all day and it was dark by the time the convoy – T4 and Defender – got moving. Both vehicles got stuck at a couple of points, but nothing major, and they finally reached camp at 11.00pm.

In total the breakdown cost the T4 crew about 18 hours and left them with around 1,200km to catch up. The stage 4 time window had been used up so they were out of their class of the rally itself, but at least now the T4 Kerax could resume its role of supporting the Wildcats.

Just to complete a stage full of surprises, Tony Harris got the shock of his life that evening when an error in the official results showed him and Cathy leading the rally! It was a moment of light relief for everyone and caused Captain Harris to be the butt of many jokes that night. A souvenir print-out would no doubt be packed into his kit for the journey home...

⬇ **Chris Ratter uses a high-pressure airbag to help lift the new transfer box into place. These bags are often used in technical rescues of heavy vehicles and can lift up to 85 tonnes**

Road sections	100km	
Special stage	243km	
Total	343km	

Car	Time	Variation	
Orange Plant	6h 40m 30s	4h 10m 16s	113th
RatCat	7h 16m 25s	4h 46m 11s	118th
Joy	7h 56m 56s	5h 26m 42s	123rd
I.R.D.	–	–	–

Truck	Time	Variation	
T4	50h	47h 4m 2s	74th

Tony Harris shows off what appeared to be a winning stage time, quicker even than eventual rally winner Stéphane Peterhansel – but this was an error!

STAGE 4 • 8 JANUARY 2013
NAZCA TO AREQUIPA

Day Four of the Dakar was sad for everyone at Race2Recovery, both for those in South America and for people at home in the UK, because the Wildcat of Tony Harris and Cathy Derousseaux was excluded and one of the other entries was forced to retire. The mechanics found I.R.D.'s retirement the more difficult in many ways, as it was a frustrating failure at too early a point in the race.

After returning to the bivouac at the end of Day Two with some question marks hanging over them, Tony and Cathy were allowed to start Day Three pending an analysis of the second day's results. An ASO Dakar committee met to discuss the car's progress and, based on that evidence, they decided that I.R.D. had not reached sufficient waypoints to be allowed to continue in the rally.

'In the back of our minds, we thought this might be a possibility,' said Tony after receiving the devastating news. 'After two years of hard work it's heart-breaking for Cathy and me, but the project has always been about the team, not individuals. We will now concentrate on the three crews left in the rally and support them as they strive to reach the finish.'

Tony's mum, Julia, knew only too well the commitment and hard work he had put into R2R and how it really was his baby. 'I feel so sorry for Tony,' said Julia, speaking from the UK. 'I know how devastated he'll be and I feel so bitterly disappointed for him and Cathy. R2R has been all he has thought about for the past two years and now it's come to this cruel end. I wish the organisers could have let them carry on to try and complete the race, even if they were not to be placed, but I know that rules have to be adhered to.'

As the news slowly sank in for Tony, the crews of the other three Wildcats still had work to do, however, and there was no time to sit and dwell on things. Day Four saw them descend a mighty dune and cross a wadi (dry river bed) during a very long stage. Some cars fared better than others. Rally favourite Robby Gordon bore the damage he'd suffered like a battle scar, arriving back at base with the front of his Hummer missing – and he's an experienced Dakar veteran. Not even the best come away unscathed.

After 200km driving southwards and nearly three hours on the road, Tom Neathway informed Quin Evans that the Orange Plant car had stopped on the stage

with a fuel problem. More news then filtered through from Ben Gott that the RatCat had also stopped, having lost all-wheel drive when a propshaft failed.

Quin, in the team management's 'Green Leader' Discovery, did a rapid calculation and decided that, with two cars in trouble, he needed to get close to their location. He contacted Tony via sat phone. Tony was way to the south of Green Leader's now static position and so Quin instructed him to return to 'RV' (rendezvous) with the mechanics' Discovery, 'Slider', at an agreed piste/road crossing point. Tony still had a fully serviceable 4x4 system and if, by some miracle, he could RV with Ben, then I.R.D. could act as a propshaft donor to RatCat. Meanwhile, under Quin's instructions, 'Green Leader' turned round and Team Manager Andrew 'Pav' Taylor drove 180km north, back the way they had just come. The Discovery was now running directly against the flow of traffic because the remaining race teams were all still heading south – rush hour in the desert!

Tony and I.R.D. had managed to find the aforementioned road section and were ready to assist in recovery if required. Ben was able to spot I.R.D. in the road with his headlights and fairly quickly he fitted the replacement propshaft and was off after Matt. The key question on everyone's lips, however, was whether Ben now had enough time to get through the horrendous dunes before the stage was closed and he was timed out.

Mission accomplished, Quin climbed aboard 'Green

⬆ Robby Gordon's battered Hummer (top) powers on to complete the stage despite flipping right over earlier in the day; the Orange Plant car (bottom) demonstrates the awesome power the Wildcat delivers

Leader' again and it turned south to retrace its steps and rejoin the rally. The distance displayed on the trip computer to the next bivouac at Arequipa was 460km – after they'd already travelled over 400km during the day. But as the Discovery pulled away in the darkness, the sat phone trilled once again. This time it was Justin and Tom who had solved their fuel problem but had terminally destroyed their Orange Plant car by damaging the transfer box, which in turn had torn a hole in the gearbox and this, in turn, broke the differential.

The T4 support crew were once again pointed back to Justin and Tom – this time stuck on the other side of a flooded river. Without too much hassle the Orange Plant car was recovered and towed to a tarmac road where the T5 support team could descend on it and try to effect a repair or take it to the next bivouac. Sadly, on this occasion the damage was terminal and the Dakar adventure was over for Justin and Tom. It was also a bitter pill for the T4 crew after enduring a 1,200km drive to make up the deficit after their stoppage, as they came over the Stage 5 timing line just 30 minutes after deadline – there would be no more special stages for the Kerax.

'We're distraught at not being able to continue in the rally and get Gordon's car to the finish line,' said Tom. 'We felt very passionate about the fact that we wanted to get

🏴 **A disappointed Cathy Derousseaux retires from her Dakar adventure**

🏴 **Tony Harris rings home with disappointing news**

to the finish in Gordon's memory, given the donation of the car from his family after he passed away. On a personal note, I'm gutted that after all our training and hard work we have had to retire, but I hope our efforts in the build-up and during our four days of racing have helped to inspire other people to challenge themselves, no matter what their disability, illness or adverse circumstances.'

The sun started to set over the bivouac, but there was still no sign of any R2R cars. Then, just as darkness fell and the cameras were being packed away for another day, the telltale roar of a V8 could be heard across the valley. Two headlights were spotted, and then four, and minutes later the two Wildcats came into view. As the cars motored home there was some good news to end the day – the T4 support truck, after its mammoth journey and being stranded in the dunes, apart from the rest of the team for days, was finally en route back to camp.

'It's been a quite a day and there'll be no respite tomorrow as the Dakar leaves Peru and heads to Chile,' said Pav. 'At the risk of repeating myself, this has been another harsh day but there's no such thing as "easy" out here. We've come here for the ultimate automotive challenge, so none of this is a surprise.'

STAGE 4
NAZCO TO AREQUIPA

Road sections	429km
Special stage	288km
Total	717km

Car	Time	Variation	
Orange Plant	16h	12h 31m 14s	122nd
RatCat	16h	12h 31m 14s	124th
Joy	16h 20m	12h 51m 14s	128th
I.R.D.	–	–	–

Truck	Time	Variation	
T4	–	–	–

US Marines Tim Read (left) and Mark Zambon (right) genning up at the camp

STAGE 5 • 9 JANUARY 2013
AREQUIPA TO ARICA

Day Five was a horrific day for the Race2Recovery team, and it nearly saw them pull out of the rally completely. Three team members – John Winskill, Lee Townsend and Justin Birchall – were badly injured when their support vehicle was involved in a road traffic accident with a local taxi and another civilian vehicle, tragically resulting in two fatalities.

The head-on collision happened late in the evening while the support team were on the liaison route near the Peru–Chile border crossing at Arica. The R2R men were all transferred to a local hospital and later flown to hospital in Lima where their condition was described as 'stable and conscious'.

Team leader Tony Harris said: 'Our hearts go out to families and relatives of those who have died in this tragic accident and we offer them our sympathy and heartfelt condolences. The team have discussed at length whether we should continue under the circumstances, but we have unanimously agreed to stay in the challenge with the two remaining Wildcats. This is a huge shock, but we know

that we have the blessing of the injured and they want the team to finish.'

It was difficult for the crews of the two surviving Wildcats to carry on after the hearing the news, but Ben and Mark returned safely to camp after a great run, as did Matt and Barney, despite being plagued by continuing overheating problems with Joy.

⬆ **The T5s parked up during one of the enforced rest periods**

⬇ **Mark and Ben learning how to stick the RatCat into the yellow jaws**

⬇ The team quickly took control at the accident scene, applying their military skills to emergency rescue and triage in ways they would not have imagined hours earlier

⬆ The T4 powers through one of the liaison stages

STAGE 5
AREQUIPA TO ARICA

Road sections	337km
Special stage	172km
Total	509km

Car	Time	Variation	
RatCat	3h 15m 43s	1h 26m 3s	99th
Joy	7h	5h 10m 20s	122nd
Orange Plant	–	–	–
I.R.D.	–	–	–

Truck	Time	Variation	
T4	100h	97h 52m 26s	69th

RACE2RECOVERY
THE CRASH

John Winskill's account

The screaming noise of crunching metal, imploding glass and ripping steel was unbearable. A second pair of headlights swerved and rocketed past my door pillar. The driver of a blue vehicle was desperately wrestling for control as he came through the debris. He disappeared out of my vision off to the right.

Then silence. The Defender engine was not running. I heard a quiet whimper in the back and a rasping, pained noise.

To my left, Lee stirred and I saw his pale face looking across, eyes wide and terrified.

'Lee, Justin… talk to me… fellas… you gotta talk to me. Justin, are you okay? Lee are you okay?'

Lee's voice was calm but he was clearly in great pain. 'I've broken my leg, I can feel blood everywhere… I think I've broken my leg!' Justin's response was far more worrying. 'I can't breathe…' were the only words he could utter – clutching his chest, his face deathly white. I knew we had to get in contact with the front Discoveries and have them turn round.

I could see steam pouring from the ruptured Land Rover – what had been the engine bay was now fully exposed to the evening air. The car's coolant mixed with oils was leaking out from its destroyed engine compartment on to the road. In what remained of the cabin area I could make out what looked like a misshapen blanket, draped across the interior of the car like a lumpy shroud.

Flashes filled the cab, endless white strobes with no rhythm or pattern to them, staccato blazes of pure brilliance followed by darkness once again. I wondered briefly if this was the start of the much-fabled 'white tunnel of light' to lands beyond life. I was rapidly aroused from this thought by a small voice at the chasm, where the driver's door had once been. 'Tranquillo, tranquillo,' the voice said, as it tried to calm us. A garbled Spanish instruction and the flashes

⬆ **The damaged Defender 130**   ⬇ **John Winskill**

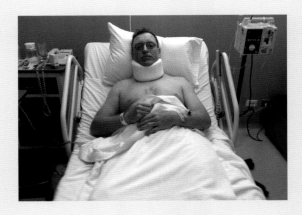

immediately ceased. I started to shout 'Ambulancia, ambulancia' in reply, which I hoped was a passable Spanish translation.

Then I heard a voice that seemingly came out of nowhere.

I closed my eyes and then reopened them to make sure I wasn't imagining it. The unmistakable tones of Marty Rae could be heard shouting instructions at Baz Whittingham, who calmly drew a Leatherman from his waist belt and, carefully holding me against the seat, sliced the cross belt in a single cut. Pav Taylor, the team manager, was with Baz and Marty and he took my hand and gently said, 'It's okay, mate, we're here. Tell me where the pain is, John. Where does it hurt?' I tried but failed to hold back the tears and 'Pav, it's my neck' was all I could muster in reply.

I felt the warmth of Pav's hands on my neck and knew he was desperately hoping we'd all be okay. I could hear his words of encouragement to Justin, who was now beginning to breathe a little more easily, and from my left I could hear Marty assessing Lee's injury. 'Lee – it's Marty. What do you reckon you've done, mate?' Lee's response that he thought he'd broken his leg led to the first light moment since the accident when Marty said, 'Lee, it's difficult to tell whether you've got a badly swollen leg, suggesting a compound break, or whether you've just got fat legs, mate!', which brought a quiet, controlled snigger from Mark Cullum, who was now entrusted with securing my spine.

By now crowds had really gathered. The TV crew and the Peruvian rescue teams had also arrived and the blue lights reflecting from the debris on the ground announced that at least one ambulance was here. It was decided by Marty that the order of extraction would be me first, on a spinal board, and then Lee, who it transpired was actually pinned to the vehicle by his feet, which had been trapped when the Defender bulkhead had been driven inwards by the collision. Justin was already clear of the wreck and was sitting on the grass verge.

Under the control of the French ASO doctor, as well as Marty and Mark, the crews fought to slide the board down between my back and the Defender seat. I screamed as Mark tried to secure my neck and prevent me from writhing too much. Eventually I was drawn rearwards and out of the Defender by the back passenger door.

Before the ambulance doors closed Mark Cullum, Pav and Marty wished us well and then, after what seemed like an eternity, the ambulance drew up in the ER bay at Tacna hospital. The French medical team took control and instructed the Peruvian doctors to provide pain relief and examine my injuries. I was relieved to see Justin and Lee drawn up in beds next to mine.

It was then that I learned the seriousness of the accident. Chris Ratter leaned across and in hushed whispers explained to me that my blood had been tested for traces of alcohol, something that was mandatory in the case of an RTA in which there were multiple fatalities. This news hit me like a block of ice, and I suddenly realised that the misshapen blanket I'd seen draped across the front seat of the light-coloured vehicle was, in fact, that vehicle's driver. Once again the tears flowed as the enormity of the situation filtered through my pain.

Other recollections

Whilst this accident was surely another blow for the team in terms of their sequence of bad luck, front passenger Lee Townsend recounted what he considered as more positive luck. 'When I first opened my eyes after the impact the first thing I saw was another car coming straight for us before he turned away at the last minute, just missing us again. Also the fact that the 600kg transfer box we had in the back came out the side of the pick-up and not through the back where it would most likely have killed us.'

'It has been an incredibly testing time for us all,' said Pav Taylor the following day. 'I was first on the scene with Marty and it really was a horrifying sight. The military guys were fantastic and just went into autopilot; some of the civilians found the whole thing very hard, which was understandable. When we got to the hospital it was pure chaos. We needed translators to help us with the statements

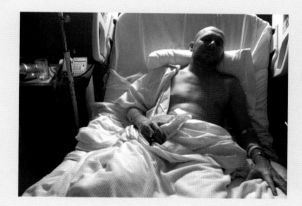

↑ Justin Birchall   ↓ Lee Townsend

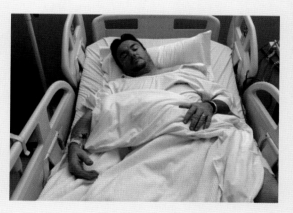

as they had to be read and checked. I then had to sort out the embassy queries and insurance policies, and also make sure the families back in the UK were fully informed of the situation.'

Over to Quin Evans: 'Today, the military guys came into their own. All their training kicked in instinctively and it really was very impressive. They took control of the situation in a calm and controlled manner, which is exactly what was needed.'

Marty Rae: 'I was one of the first on the scene and assessed the situation. I wasn't prepared for what I saw and, even by my standards, it shocked me. Justin was an instant concern to me, Lee was his usual calm self despite the horror around him, and Pav was looking after John. People were being reassured and I was happy that everyone was getting the attention they needed.

'I went and had a look at the other car and saw that three were injured, two were deceased and four people were on the floor but had clear airways. My priority was to get the local woman and Justin to hospital first. I escorted them to the hospital and I had no further participation in the Dakar after that day but I don't regret my decision – it was the right thing to do and I wanted to be there.

'In the hospital I was very busy, dealing with the embassy, being the clinic staff liaison and even a shopper as I had to get a cab to the local department store to buy clothes for myself and also the guys who had come in wearing just their underwear.

'At the accident scene I took John's seat in the wrecked 130 and tried to free Lee from the seat. Lee told me I was bending him in ways he shouldn't be bent. A fireman started to cut out Lee from the outside, and another of the firemen was reading the instructions to his 'jaws of life' prior to using them, which was a bit worrying. They made the first cut which shorted out the battery and filled the car with smoke. Lee was still stuck and the fire extinguishers that had been mounted in the car had crushed on impact...

I raced and got a fire extinguisher from my car and sat next to Lee, keeping him calm. Mark Cullum, a fully trained fireman, showed the fire brigade the quickest way to free Lee with the help of a reporter translating. Lee was the last casualty to be put in the ambulance and the whole experience seemed only to take about five minutes but in reality it was more like an hour...'

STAGE 6 · 10 JANUARY 2013
ARICA TO CALAMA

Bad things happen in threes, or so we are told, and this was confirmed on Stage Six. Surely the team now deserved a little bit of good fortune to see them through the second half of the rally?

Ben Gott and Mark Zambon started the stage still reeling from news of the accident the day before, but they were even more determined to get to the finish. It wasn't long before their minds were focused elsewhere. Just after they'd crested a dune they saw a local truck coming out of nowhere, beeping its horn madly but not slowing

down, and within seconds it rammed into the back of the Wildcat. The left-rear corner now bore a sizeable war wound, but luckily there was no serious damage.

'It could have been much worse,' admitted Ben. 'In a single smack, your Dakar dream can be over.'

Sadly for Mark and Ben these words, spoken at the midway point of the sixth stage, proved prophetic. On the following section of the special stage they hit a ditch at considerable speed and rolled several times, taking themselves out of the event for good.

⬇ **The T4 crew assisting Ben Gott and Mark Zambon just hours before their eventful evening**

← RatCat digs her claws into the dunes racing for the end of the stage

'The RatCat's retirement is so infuriating as Ben and Mark had the experience and skills to finish but a random ditch has put an end to that,' said Chris Astles afterwards.

Ben requested immediate medical assistance, using the in-car safety system, and aid soon arrived. Medical professionals were scrambled and a Dutch support truck helped them to escape from the car.

'We were travelling at about 60mph,' Mark said. 'It was a big accident, but we're okay and there was actually a funny moment. When the Dutch guys pulled me out, one of my legs fell off and the guy panicked! I had to tell him they were prosthetic!' Mark was taken for observation to the medical centre at the event

↑ The RatCat showing her battle scars after being nerfed by a rogue race truck

'We were travelling at about 60mph. It was a big accident, but we're okay.'

Mark Zambon

The Dakar punishes all creatures great and small – the De Rooy Team truck of Hans Stacey limps into the bivouac

bivouac, but fortunately he'd only suffered bruising.

'The large square-edged wash-out ditch was coming straight for us and we couldn't miss it,' said Ben. 'I tried to slow down as much as possible but we still hit it hard, with my corner going first, and then we punched the far bank and fired up into the air. The windscreen came out with the force of the impact and Mark was rescued through that, with the help of the Dutch truck crew. The RatCat was damaged beyond repair, although I didn't know it at this point, but I soon realised there was something seriously wrong with me – my back was rock solid and I was in agony.

'The medical staff thought I had broken my back or had fractured vertebrae – it was now getting scary, and I was going through in my mind what the future would hold for me if the worst-case scenario became a reality. Thankfully, after more tests (in a local hospital in Calama), I was told I was fine and a few hours later I was discharged. It was a shock for everyone and I still can't believe it. I was flown to the next bivouac in the Andes on a Chilean Air Force plane which was cool and only took an hour. The rest of the guys would spend a good ten hours minimum driving and up and over the mountains. It felt very strange being away from everybody else and I was still in a lot of pain and had had no sleep, with a morphine comedown – I felt like a tramp walking around with my bag of cut-up race suit, a passport and a dead phone!'

The retirement of the third car was another huge blow for the team, but it was not all over by any stretch of the imagination. Joy was still very much in the running and co-driver Barney was still smiling. 'Our car, Joy, overheats in the sun so we're having to do the Dakar in the dark,' he said. 'It's frustrating but we won't give up – we're going to make it to that finish line. We have everyone behind us and the team spirit is fantastic.'

Cathy works through the not-so-glamorous side of international motorsport – checking team passports

↑ The Dakar's
lady of the night
passing a waypoint

De Rooy suffered a monster crash to match his Iveco monster truck, proving the Dakar makes no exception for experience or budgets.

'It has been a baptism of fire and we've experienced everything that goes hand-in-hand with the Dakar Rally,' said team manager 'Pav' Taylor. 'We can now testify that it's the toughest race in the world. The team has performed in an outstanding way, given the scale of the challenge, and everyone has put in hours and hours of hard graft, no matter whether it's day or night.'

Everyone was buoyed up by the good news that the team members who'd been injured in the accident were making progress in Peru.

However, there were nearly tears for Joy as Matt explained: 'I got my sums wrong tonight and we ran out of fuel with about 80km of the special stage to go. Another competitor stopped to tell us that another car like ours had crashed and we knew it was Mark and Ben. He said they were

The Race2Recovery team were not alone in withdrawals on this stage. Veteran Spanish rally driver Carlos Sainz of the Qatar Red Bull Team retired with engine problems in his Demon Jeffries Buggy and Hans Stacey of the Petronas Team

☚ Having just taken a break, Matt and
Barney look refreshed for the next run!

only about 1km ahead so I decided to run with a torch. I could see a flashing beacon but then it disappeared and I had nowhere to aim for. It was also a lot further than the 1km the guy had said – more like 8km. I was so hot from running by this point and couldn't find my bearings. I borrowed a motorbike that had been left unattended on the roadside and had to take my top off as I was sweating so much.

'I got completely lost but luckily a bunch of magnificently moustached and jovial Argentine T2 guys found me. They said they could only make room for me if I would speak to the Queen and promise the return of the Falkland Islands! Before I knew it, we were all squeezed in and heading back to Joy. It was an insane evening and the longest time Barney and I had been apart – four hours!'

By some strange stroke of luck, the recovered RatCat had been refuelled not long before and the T4 crew transferred virtually a tankful into Joy.

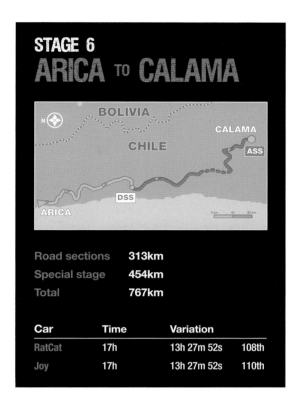

STAGE 6
ARICA TO CALAMA

Road sections	**313km**	
Special stage	**454km**	
Total	**767km**	

Car	Time	Variation	
RatCat	17h	13h 27m 52s	108th
Joy	17h	13h 27m 52s	110th

⬇ Tom Neathway and Tim Read talk prosthetics

STAGE 7 · 11 JANUARY 2013
CALAMA TO SALTA

The accident, retirement and exclusion all underlined just how much of a team game the Dakar Rally really is, and how team morale was paramount if the dream of crossing the line was to be realised.

Twenty-eight people were involved in Race2Recovery on the Dakar, and although much of the spotlight had been on the racing pairs, the mechanics were tested to their limits too. They had a nocturnal schedule, working through the night to prepare the cars for the next stage, and trying to sleep in the team's support trucks and Land Rover Discoveries as they were driven from bivouac to bivouac. It was a strange, nomadic and hugely demanding existence and certainly not for the faint-hearted.

All the attention was now on the one remaining Wildcat, Joy, and its crew, Barney Gillespie and Matt O'Hare. Joy was confirmed as having finished Stage Six and passed through the time control to signal its start on Stage Seven, first travelling on the liaison route before tackling the timed 220km special stage. It wasn't an easy feat as the car still had to travel through the

night because of problems with the fuel vaporising under the fierce heat of the sun during the day. Joy made it with very little time left on the clock.

The heat was a major factor with temperatures hitting 40°C. It was vital that everyone in the team stayed hydrated, which was easier said than done when the guys hardly had a spare minute to close their eyes let alone drink a bottle of water. A couple of the non-military guys found the heat particularly harsh

⬆ **Tony using the Peltor headset to conduct a radio interview on the rally**

⬇ **The Gaucho film crew at the Argentinian/ Chilean border**

at times and had to be reminded constantly to keep drinking. Nagging on occasion became second nature to the military men but only because they had the best interests of the team in mind.

'I don't know how we're keeping going, to be honest,' said Barney. 'But on we go and we will make it, you'll see.'

Altitude reared its ugly head on this stage as Joy had to travel 715km across the Andes in Argentina, climbing to between 3,500–4,000m, where temperatures now dropped to an average 15°C and, yes, there was plenty of snow to be seen as the whole rally convoy for the liaison stage finished at the remarkable height of 4,975m. Barney and Matt are relatively fit and have spent most of their lives passing fitness tests and being pushed physically, but none of this helps when altitude takes hold. Some of the team suffered with sickness. When the T5 MAN truck broke down at over 4,200m above sea level, Tim Read was affected badly, vomiting every few minutes and suffering bad headaches too; thankfully, after about five hours his body adjusted to the environment.

Altitude doesn't just affect the body. The reduction in oxygen puts more strain on an engine as it cannot burn fuel as efficiently. More fuel is used to provide less power, resulting in a reduction in maximum speed of some 20–50kph.

Joy was never going to make it easy for the lads to drive her across the line. She'd shown her temperamental nature before she even landed in South America, when she broke down in France – which might not have been a good omen – but she was the only car still in the race. Day Seven was no different as she continued to suffer fuelling problems en route, but the guys made it to the bivouac at 2.00am. The mechanics immediately set to work, cutting holes in the bonnet and the rear clam shell to try and resolve the overheating problems, while Matt and Barney snatched some much-needed sleep.

Sad news from the French camp confirmed that one of their riders, Thomas Bourgin, aged 25, was tragically killed as he made his way to the start of the stage. He'd collided with a Chilean police car travelling in the opposite direction on a road section. Pav spoke for everyone when he said, 'We are very sad to hear this news and express our most sincere condolences to Thomas's family and friends.'

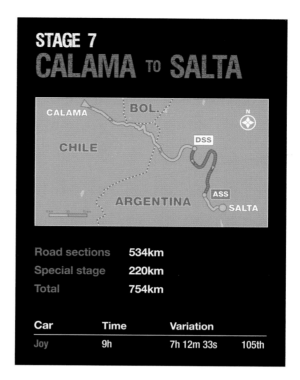

STAGE 7
CALAMA TO SALTA

Road sections	534km
Special stage	220km
Total	754km

Car	Time	Variation	
Joy	9h	7h 12m 33s	105th

⬇ Mark Zambon showing his enthusiasm hadn't waned after a week on the Dakar; the altimeter in the film crew's Discovery showing the highest stage of the rally

STAGE 8 • 12 JANUARY 2013
SALTA TO TUCUMAN

This was supposed to be another monster day for Joy and the support crew, but rain soon set in and washed away the jeopardy. The special stage was cut short by flash floods and the team had no choice but to retire to the bivouac in Tucumán, in spirits as high as the altitude. An unexpected intervention by Mother Nature had allowed some very weary heads the chance of a rest.

After getting back to the bivouac the night before, Ben Gott was tasked with going to the aid of the MAN Kat, which was still stuck at high altitude having lost drive. A four-hour journey in the support Discoveries

⬆ Mark Zambon and Martyn Williams at the Tucumán bivouac
– Mark accounting for fuel expenses while Martyn checks in on Facebook via the Inmarsat satellite communication system

brought Ben, Quin Evans, Baz Whittingham and Sean Whatley to the stricken T5. It looked like the vehicle had been driven with the exhaust brake on; the exhaust brake closes off the exhaust path from the engine, compressing the gases and as there is no fuel being applied, the engine creates a braking effect, slowing down the vehicle. But after a full drain, clean of filter and renewal of oil – all 36 litres – she came back to life. All looked good and everyone set off again to go to the next night's bivouac looking forward to the rest day.

The chance to rest couldn't come soon enough for all of them. Ben sacrificed his chance to quench his thirst in order to keep awake in the driving seat. After 37 hours of driving before the second day's stage and then his accident, it got to the point where he was falling asleep at the wheel, so he used his water to pour over his head and down the back of his neck to shock his eyes open again. USN energy gels, energy drinks and cat-napping were also solutions to the team's sleep deprivation.

STAGE 8
SALTA ᴛᴏ TUCUMAN

Road sections	379km
Special stage	470km
Total	849km

Car	Time	Variation	
Joy	2h 7m 21s	12m 15s	105th

⬇ Tim Read tinkers with Joy as she continued to battle the heat

RACE2RECOVERY
THE BIVOUAC

The bivouac is very difficult to describe adequately. In terms of its size, noise, smells and constant action it is an experience in itself.

It's a temporary safe haven for exhausted drivers, navigators and assistance teams each day. Loosely based on a US city plan of blocks and avenues, the bivouac site measures approximately a kilometre by a kilometre. Usually sited off a main metalled road but far enough into the desert to appear remote, this expanse of reclaimed sand is a very welcome sight for all as they arrive after another exhausting day spent battling endless dunes, river valleys, gravel tracks and hard-packed race piste.

Occupying such a site takes hours of planning and rehearsal but no two bivouac set-ups are identical. The Race2Recovery team, led by their bivouac advance party of John Winskill, Dave Reeve, Jonny Koonja and Tim Read in the Defender 130, and followed by Chris Astles and Sean Whatley in the 'Duff' and Gareth Paterson, Martyn Williams and Rick Nixon in the MAN Kat T5, would always arrive at the site ahead of the rest of the R2R team including, of course, the race vehicles.

In order to access the site and get past the very heavy security and military guards, they would have their electronic wrist bands scanned and then follow the inimitable 'monkey bike' ridden by a goggle-wearing ASO man, through the avenues and blocks to the intended location.

The key role of the bivouac is to provide mechanical support for the T1 cars and the T4 truck, and so Dave Reeve, Sean Whatley and Rick Nixon were first in to judge the lie of the land.

Any inclines or unevenness could prove disastrous for a Wildcat's underbelly ramp system and so the three mechanics establish the correct orientation for the service bay areas. The T5 trucks were then brought in and placed on either extremity of the R2R site.

Once in location, the T5s would deposit their box bodies on to the sand in order to provide easy access to the massive stores and logistics spares for the disabled guys. The very next area to be set up was the Command and Control (C2) Easy Up. This was often rigged at the cab end of the T5 MAN truck to enable power to be drawn from the on-board generator.

This power was then routed to a ten-way supply box to provide the necessary 'juice' through UK-type three-pin sockets for laptops, sat phone chargers and radio base stations, and also provided some spare sockets for team members to plug in their personal phone chargers. Most importantly, this C2 area, with its trestle tables and bench seats, provided the critical shade needed for the assistance teams to shelter from the incredibly powerful sun during the day and for the navigators and drivers to have somewhere to sit down at night and work through their all-important road book for the following day's stage.

Next to be set up was the accommodation tentage. With 28 team members and five fellas from the Gaucho TV crew,

⬇ Jonny Koonja and Chris and Phill Bayliss discuss
mechanical issues with team manager Pav

⬇ Hydration is vital on the rally with temperatures in excess of 40°C
and high humidity. Water was supplied for all teams at every bivouac

33 tents had to be erected each day. This was easy as the tents were the standard pop-up type so it was simply a matter of unzipping a bag and throwing the tent into the air and catching it again before the ever-present prevailing wind caught it. Each person had their own tent as it was decided that, after as much as 18 hours a day locked in various vehicles together, personal space was essential for at least some of the time.

The T1 crews all had tents next to each other and the logistics team ensured that the disabled guys had the easiest access to their tents. For example, Tom Neathway's tent was always at the end of a row and normally next to the C2 area. Therefore, the first line of tents furthest from the service bay areas invariably accommodated the 11 drivers and co-drivers (eight from the Wildcats and three from the T4). The next row up was generally logistics people, team management and TV crews. The third and final row was often the mechanics, so that their tents could be nearest the cars they were working on, and when their work was complete (often close to dawn) they could collapse quickly into their individual tents.

Although erecting the tents was easy, taking them down was a nightmare. With a quick referral to the online video from the manufacturer, the black art was learnt by a few, and eventually the 'tent team' of John Winskill, Tim Read and Baz Whittingham could get a tent down and in its bag in about 90 seconds! For 33 tents the task still took over an hour and was never easy in the heat and dust.

Under each vehicle Easy Up shelter, the team laid down tarpaulins for the cars to park on. These 'tarps' enabled the mechanics to crawl around under the car without too much fear of scorpion stings or getting burnt by the super-heated sand, and also allowed the recovery of the inevitably dropped bolt or washer.

The area at the end of the R2R encampment was reserved for the assistance cars. The four Discoveries would reverse line abreast and close one end of the pitch. This had two benefits. Firstly, it acted as a wind break to cut off the horizontal dust devils that often formed in the bivouac area. Secondly, for safety, the Discoveries acted as a physical barrier between the R2R encampment and the endless traffic that prowled around the site all day and night.

Routine in the bivouac, once established, was pretty well ingrained in all from an early stage. Hydration was key to all and Marty 'Bivouac Sergeant Major' Rae reminded all that drinking fluid was a good thing. Each team member had a USN drinks container that they could mix up with energy supplements and powders to make the fluid a little more palatable. The supply of chilled water in 500ml bottles either came from the ASO feeding marquees or from R2R's own fridge systems carried in each support car, and inside the T5 box bodies. The military guys on the team were well versed in the need for hydration given experiences in Iraq and Afghanistan, but the civilian team members sometimes needed some gentle reminding.

Feeding was in the Dakar 2013 communal 'cook-house' marquees. The food was generally terrific but spaghetti bolognese for breakfast raised a few eyebrows.

The feeding marquees were non-denominational, with no area specifically set aside for the big teams. You could find yourself passing Carols Sainz a bread roll, while having your tray bumped by Robbie Gordon at the same time as Stéphane Peterhansel was filling his flask from the hot water point.

Showers and chemical toilets were adjacent to the feeding area, and while effective, were certainly far from luxurious. The key was timing and R2R rapidly found that 4am was the best time for ablutions!

⬇ **Tom Neathway and Tim Read carry on with military precision; used to looking after their weapons, they pay the same close attention to their prosthetics**

⬇ **Charlie Sincock surveys the T5 MAN Kat at Córdoba bivuoac**

RACE2RECOVERY
DAKAR REST DAY

⬆ It may be called a 'rest day' but the truth was far from it as the bivoauc was a hive of activity

The event's ninth day was the only rest day and a chance for the team to regroup, sleep, work on the one remaining car and strategically plan for the second week of racing. A decent night's sleep was the first priority for everyone, apart from the mechanics, as the following day would see the longest special stage in the rally (593km), in temperatures likely to soar to over 45°C.

'I'm delighted for the team that we have reached rest day,' said Ben Gott. 'Everyone had the chance for a bit of a catch-up and I was thrilled that Matt and Barney had made it to the milestone of the halfway point, but seeing only three cars in our camp and walking around watching everyone prepping for the second half of the rally really hurts.'

➡ Sponsors lose out to Tim Read's power tools in creating extra venting for Joy

There were 450 vehicles entered the 2013 Dakar, comprising 183 motorbikes, 40 quad bikes, 152 cars and 75 trucks. At the end of the first week, which had seen crews travel between 4,330km and 4,550km, the number that had dropped out of the event stood at 110 (24%). Of these, 70 were withdrawn, 33 didn't make a specific stage start time and seven were disqualified.

At this halfway stage Wildcat Joy was showing last overall in the cars' category, but as the aim was to finish, that didn't matter. The fact that Race2Recovery were even there, representing people with disabilities and achieving the extraordinary, was the important thing.

For most people, Sundays are a rest day, the one day of the week to read the paper, have brunch and watch the world go by, but not if you're a mechanic whose team is competing in the Dakar. They were hard at work from the early hours, trying to fix the problems that had blighted Joy's progress throughout the week.

'We had a huge list of things to do,' said mechanic Sean Whatley. 'On the Dakar you've got limited resources so you need to adopt some lateral thinking. We've done everything we can to improve the cooling for the fuel system – even scavenging parts from our retired cars to improve the efficiency of the radiators. Joy has new oil and new tyres and she's ready to crack on.'

The overheating problems were tackled in as many ways as possible. A fuel-cooling radiator was put in the fuel line. The water radiator was replaced with the one from the Orange Plant car and the two fans from that car were also fitted as they were working more effectively. A fan was fitted in the gearbox tunnel to keep the fuel pumps cool. The fuel pumps were wrapped in foam and a windscreen washer jet was plumbed into a water supply to provide some cooling effect through the foam; there was a button for Barney to press to activate the jet.

⬇ Andrew Kentigern-Fox took time out to visit the team on the South American leg of his world tour

A FAN TURNS UP

Andrew Kentigern-Fox contacted the team early in 2012 to say that he was doing a world tour on his BMW motorcycle. He offered to put a Race2Recovery sticker on the bike and send pictures from various exotic locations. Then, late in 2012, he arrived in South America and embarked on the Dakar rally route, hoping to reach the finish line in Santiago before the team. Between Christmas and New Year he contacted the team again to say that the miles in Argentina were passing by very slowly. His goal had changed and he was now aiming to meet them on the rest day at San Miguel Tucumán and take pictures. He made it and spent a week enjoying the Dakar's unique atmosphere – and also provided the team with amazing photographs, some of which are used here in the book.

↑ Tim Hare works
through the 'to do' list...

↑ Members of Race2Recovery meet with Nasser
Al-Attiyah and crew from the Qatar Red Bull Team

⬆ Matt's and Barney's second skins
also get the chance for a wash and rest

BACK IN THE UK

As Race2Recovery's social media manager, Debbie Harrison was kept very busy looking after five accounts – Google+, Facebook, twitter, YouTube and Pinterest – through the build-up to the Dakar and, of course, during the event itself.

It was especially frenetic on 3 January, two days before the start, when she supported the twitter campaign run by R2R's PR agency, Fast Track. By midday the R2R hashtag #beyondinjury had generated 5.4 million impressions and the most from a single tweet was 1.7 million courtesy of Chelsea FC.

During the Dakar, Debbie provided a live news feed for 12–15 hours a day, helped by Alec Savery. While Alec tracked the Wildcats' progress, Debbie kept the social media accounts updated and interacted with followers and families. As the rally drew to a close there were also many questions from the public that Debbie endeavoured to answer individually.

Before the event Debbie set up a closed group on Facebook for family members of the team to share information, questions and concerns privately. As she explains, 'The group was often referred to as the "WAGs" although we also had parents and children, and everyone was addressed as "Ladies" although we had a few men. As the rally progressed this group became a vital source of support, uniting families from across the UK and the US. The group became essential after the road accident, particularly for the families of the three team members who were seriously injured. I had to work hard to make sure families had enough information to reassure them, but I also had to make it explicit that they couldn't share this information until the facts had been established.'

When Ben Gott and Mark Zambon crashed out of the Dakar, Debbie also liaised with Ben's partner in the UK and Mark's wife in the US. 'While they were waiting in the desert for medical assistance, I remained online and at one point it looked as if Mark would be left alone in the dark, in the desert with no-one for miles around. I was able to remind his wife Marta that although he was now an amputee, he was also a Marine and he would cope.'

Through social media Debbie also communicated closely with sponsors and with Help for Heroes and Tedworth House to keep them informed and involved, and also liaised constantly with the R2R fundraising manager Tiff Hyde to maximise the fundraising campaign. Midway through the Dakar, Tiff and some dedicated R2R supporters attended Autosport International, a four-day exhibition at Birmingham's NEC where the team had displayed their driving skills in a Wildcat the previous year. 'The crowds at the Live Action show remembered them well,' said Tiff, 'and were treated to footage sent over from the Dakar – the donations came in thick and fast!'

STAGE 9 · 14 JANUARY 2013
TUCUMAN TO CORDOBA

The Dakar can lull vehicles and their crews into a false sense of security. They may experience a relatively straightforward stage, enjoy nice weather and then a perfectly timed rest day, but before long the hardest race in the world bites back and deals a punishing blow – cue Stage Nine of this year's race.

Following the day of rest, the Race2Recovery crew were faced with the longest stage of the rally. Joy would have to complete an epic 852km that included a 593km special stage, a fearsome test. But if the day's stage could be conquered, maybe, just maybe, they could start dreaming of reaching the finish...

It proved to be the hottest day so far and at 8.30am the intrepid duo of Matt and Barney in Joy emerged from the first section of the stage with smiles wreathed across their faces.

'Joy hasn't overheated once – amazing!' said a grinning Matt. 'We've actually been overtaking cars

⬇ **Joy takes to the hills with a spring in her step following her shakedown on the rest day**

for a change and it's a fantastic feeling – it might just be that we can complete the stage without driving through the night, and that would be a first for us!'

Not only did the duo have to get their heads around the arduous route but also the fact they were now minor celebrities! Joy was actually mobbed when she pulled into a filling station – it's doubtful that even Argentinean footballer Lionel Messi would have received as much attention as the two guys trying to use the pump in dirty overalls in a tired old car.

Was this going to be the first trouble-free day for the guys? Could everyone breathe a sigh of relief? Well, no, because both of the team's giant support trucks broke down en route, leaving their crews stranded by the roadside. An improvised roadside clutch change got the MAN Kat moving again, but

⬆ Joy's fan club at the local petrol station

→ Matt O'Hare relishes the new improved Joy

← Fixing the temporary airline between the donor T4 and 'The Duff'

↘ Matt and Barney being interviewed by the embedded film crew

the other, which threw a con rod and couldn't be repaired, had to be towed by the team's T4 Kerax truck for almost 300km to the bivouac. Sean Whatley and Dave Reeve had the ride of a lifetime in the broken truck as it was towed because the much larger T5 was attached to the smaller T4 by an 8ft long fixed bar. Travelling along tight and twisting roads became quite alarming as the back end of the T4 weaved from side to side. At one point, the rear end was lifted into the air, but probably the most frightening moment was when an overtaking vehicle, trying to avoid oncoming traffic, tried to pull in between the two trucks.

'As the engine had failed, Chris connected up a "bodge" airline from the Kerax to the "Duff" so we could give it the air needed to move and to brake,' explained Charlie Sincock, who drove the Kerax in this two-truck convoy. 'The brakes, however, were very strong on both trucks. If I braked in the Kerax, the "Duff" could have gone off to one side and jacked-knifed. This was extremely nerve-racking so we ended up with a brake-signalling system where I would brake twice in blipped succession if I wanted Sean to slow us both down gradually, and in an emergency I would brake just once – which happened several times when people cut me up. Sean did a brilliant job of driving for 10 hours while

only staring at my brake lights and the back of the Kerax – a truly Herculean effort.'

It's not just the cars and trucks that break down or decide to be temperamental. Tom Neathway's prosthetic right leg stopped working on this stage, due to the heat and dust.

'My prosthetics work by shifting my weight,' Tom explained. 'If I walk downhill, I put my heel down first, as an able-bodied person would, and the prosthetic reacts and also acts as a brake too as I can't control my speed. Usually I have to recharge my prosthetics back in the UK on a daily basis, so the cars had to be adapted with the necessary chargers so I could do it out in South America. It was no hardship really as when I was in the car racing, I could just plug in and the prosthetics would charge while I was sitting there – I didn't have to take them off or anything.

'However, I had real problems with them as they broke after a week and a half, so I spent the other two and half weeks on broken legs – which is unbelievably uncomfortable. I was in pain most of the time on them but you have to get on with it and not complain. They're just not used to being smashed around with all the physical work I was doing. They're made for walking on flat ground, not in heat and sand!'

If this was a Hollywood movie script, no-one would believe it...

ARGENTINA

CÓRDOBA

SAN MIGUEL
DE TUCUMÁN

DSS

ASS

Road sections	259km	
Special stage	593km	
Total	852km	

Car	Time	Variation	
Joy	9h 3m 46s	3h 27m 18s	82nd

STAGE 10 • 15 JANUARY 2013
CORDOBA TO LA RIOJA

Country & Western music was the choice of the day in Joy, and it kept Matt and Barney in good spirits driving through the Argentinean heat (in the UK, Race2Recovery fans decided that 'Stand By Your Man' should be the theme tune for Joy and the intrepid pair!). The overheating problems that had plagued the car in the first week appeared to have been alleviated too, so it was looking very promising.

'Argentina has been good to us so far,' said Matt. 'It's a beautiful country and the stages are fun. It's so hot out there, but we're loving it.'

Unfortunately, the team's eight-wheel support trucks were ruled out from playing any further part in

← Joy, thrilled to be cooling off more conventionally

➜ The local *polizia* would have no such luck to catch Joy speeding!

'This afternoon, the cameraman filming a documentary about the team looked somewhat bemused to be handed a baby for a photograph. It all happens out here on the Dakar!'

Sean Whatley, mechanic

↑ Tom Neathway resting his legs; heat and humidity gave him some trouble

⬇ Not all the property of the crew's Discovery...

↑ Tony Harris's leg stickered up

the race after breaking down in the previous day's stage. Losing the two T5s in one day was obviously a huge blow, but the guys joked at the thought of already entering the Dakar history books for the wrong reasons. How many teams have lost two support trucks in a matter of hours?

It was a busy time for the rest of the guys, who had to repack all the team's equipment into the Renault Kerax and the Land Rovers. There was some light relief, though, as signing autographs monopolised much of the lads' time, with the team's mechanics perfecting their signatures and even signing various body parts at the request of some fun-loving locals!

'This afternoon, the cameraman filming a documentary about the team looked somewhat bemused to be handed a baby for a photograph,' said mechanic Sean Whatley. 'It all happens out here on the Dakar!'

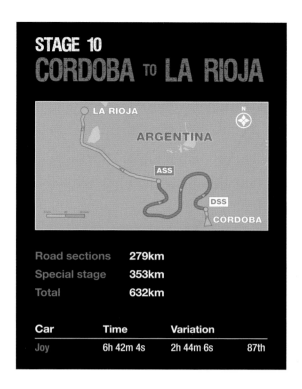

STAGE 10
CORDOBA TO LA RIOJA

Road sections	279km
Special stage	353km
Total	632km

Car	Time	Variation	
Joy	6h 42m 4s	2h 44m 6s	87th

⬇ Tony Harris on the phone with the British consulate arranging transport for the T5 DAF Drops into Chile

STAGE 11 · 16 JANUARY 2013
LA RIOJA TO FIAMBALA

Mother Nature returned in full force yet again and Stage Eleven was cancelled due to flooding. The whole rally was accordingly transported forwards a day, giving everyone time to reflect on the possibility that, as the rally was reaching its climax, the team might be granted a little good fortune and Joy would make the finish – and motorsport history too.

'I can't believe it has been cancelled – Barney and I were so looking forward to being on the dunes again!' Matt said, with perhaps a hint of sarcasm in his voice…

With three more stages to go anything could still happen, and Joy had been blighted by fuel problems since the first day.

'It somehow seems fitting that this is the last car,' continued Matt. 'There's a strong chance we'll finish, but she isn't in good health and we'll have to nurse her through. It's not in the bag by any stretch.'

The goodwill shown to Joy and her crew was nothing short of extraordinary in the latter days of the event. The boys now had a bit of a cult following and every night they caught up via their phones with what had been going on outside the Dakar bubble, reading the incredible number of messages appearing on social media outlets like Facebook, Google and Twitter.

The hash tags #TeamJoy and #allthewaytothefinish became a mantra for followers desperate for the team to complete the rally. An unconfirmed rumour was also circulating that one supporter had paid for a 'Team Joy' tattoo!

⬇ Joy gets a helping hand through the bivouac

↘ Tony Harris and Cathy Derousseaux make their way through the local petrolheads followed by one of the support Discoveries

'A family had put a painted sign outside their house in Argentina saying 'Race2Recovery real heroes'. We stopped at the sign and everyone had a photo with the family. The mother was hugging Mark and in tears – she was so happy that we had stopped. She hurried into her house and brought out glasses of water for everyone. Seeing the streets lined with people cheering you on and moments like this... I really will never forget it all.' Baz Whittingham

STAGE 11
LA RIOJA TO FIAMBALA

Road sections	262km
Special stage	219km
Total	481km

Car	Time	Variation	
Joy	1h 13m 25s	23m 4s	87th

STAGE 12 • 17 JANUARY 2013
FIAMBALA TO COPIAPO

The Race2Recovery team will never take tarmac for granted again. The 396km road sections of Day Twelve should have been a relaxing drive through some of the world's most dramatic and desolate scenery but, due to the lack of hard surfaces, the route through the mountains turned out to be as perilous as a special stage.

With altitudes approaching 5,000m, a fragile Joy and her boys faced constant jeopardy and danger. Thankfully they made it through the 'road' section, but one of the Land Rovers wasn't so lucky and now bore a war wound after being clipped by one of the competing cars.

The dreaded Dakar dunes were on the menu as well, and it was hard not to notice the concern in Matt's and Barney's eyes. Getting stuck in the soft, sandy conditions was the main worry for everyone and this was just exacerbated by a starting problem.

⬆ Joy carefully traverses the mammoth stage, climbing higher with each kilometre

⬇ Illuminated by a nearby police car, Joy steals into the night once again

A RIGHT DUFF ADVENTURE

Meanwhile the drama hadn't stopped for the rest of the Race2Recovery team: the 'Duff' had become the 'Dud' (after blowing its engine the previous day) and the MAN Kat was now being driven with effectively a crash gearbox (due to its clutch problem).

With both T5 support vehicles sidelined, the team had no option but to turn the T4 Kerax and support Discoveries into the new lightweight support unit. All spares and equipment deemed vital to get Joy to the finish were transferred to these vehicles and the T5 crews were left to limp to the port of San Antonio, Chile, for the sea voyage home.

This final journey, over sometimes impossibly winding roads, was also eventful. The T5 boys – and the Argentine driver of the lorry carrying the 'Duff' on its flat-bed trailer – had a few near misses and stoppages, particularly for low bridges and tunnels, with load heights and tyre pressures having to be adjusted on both trailer and cargo in order to squeeze beneath.

➡ The tyre pressures had to be let down on the 'Duff' to gain vital clearance on the (not so) low-loader sent to the rescue; extreme care had to be taken in gauging the right position under each tunnel and underpass for the two-day journey to Chile to meet the team's cargo ship back to Blighty

Tim Read working into
the night at the bivouac

Joy gets full attention to
ensure she makes another day

'Joy wasn't starting properly,' explained driver Matt. 'This meant we were paranoid about stalling or getting stuck in the sand. It was all about keeping the momentum going – we knew the mechanics would fix it, even if it took them most of the night. Night rolls into day here and none of us notices any more.'

While Joy was escaping the sandy jaws of the dunes and ticking off another stage, Mark Zambon and Tim Read took time out to visit Robby Gordon, the first American to win a stage of the Dakar. Gordon devotes his life to winning the rally (he finished second on this stage), but he approaches it in a slightly different way from the R2R team because he's cushioned in a world dominated by sophisticated transporters and five-star hotel rooms. He was, however, hugely impressed with the team's efforts. 'To do this event with two legs is hard enough,' he said, 'but to take it on with only one leg or even no legs is incredible. This is a badass event and these guys are doing an awesome job.'

STAGE 12
FIAMBALA TO COPIAPO

Road section	396km	
Special stage	319km	
Total	715km	

Car	Time	Variation	
Joy	8h 27m 4s	4h 50m 30s	77th

⬇ US Marines Mark Zambon and Tim Read with Speed Energy Hummer H3 countryman Robby Gordon.

STAGE 13 · 18 JANUARY 2013
COPIAPO TO LA SERENA

Dripping with money and powering through the soaring temperatures, the multi-million-dollar trucks of the corporate giants were seen riding the crest of the dunes, led by Robby Gordon's Hummer. It looked like a scene out of *Transformers*. Then the front-running trucks arrived, looking as incongruous as ever as they roared their way up the giant sand castles. There was no sign of Joy…

The team waited and waited for the familiar sound of Joy's V8 engine, cameras at the ready, and then came the faint sound of her tired engine. She emerged out of the dust and, before there was time to breathe a sigh of relief, she had gulped another litre of fuel and vanished once again into the yellow sand.

Even on this penultimate stage of the rally there was no let-up, and when Joy exited the special stage at 11.30pm, team manager 'Pav' Taylor summed up everyone's feelings: 'It's been a long hard day but we've ticked off another special stage. As I talk, we are in camp waiting for the car's return and we'll work as long as it takes to get her in the best possible condition for tomorrow's final stage. The Dakar can bite at any time and we're not getting complacent; we've come this far and tomorrow we will be ready for the final push.'

← After almost two weeks of the most arduous terrain on the planet, the pace doesn't slow for the Monster Energy MAN truck team

← Hervé Toscano in his Chevrolet Springbok on his second Dakar, hoping to cross the finish line after withdrawing in 2010 on stage 3

'The Dakar can bite at any time and we're not getting complacent.'

Andrew 'Pav' Taylor, team manager

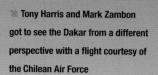

Tony Harris and Mark Zambon got to see the Dakar from a different perspective with a flight courtesy of the Chilean Air Force

Matt and Barney taking a well-earned breather

STAGE 13
COPIAPO TO LA SERENA

Road sections	294km	
Special stage	441km	
Total	735km	

Car	Time	Variation	
Joy	10h 30m	6h 49m 7s	92nd

STAGE 14 • 19 JANUARY 2013
LA SERENA TO SANTIAGO

History was made – they did it! The Race2Recovery team became the first ever disability team to complete the Dakar Rally, the toughest race in the world, when the Land Rover Defender-based Wildcat race vehicle Joy and her crew of Matt O'Hare and Phillip 'Barney' Gillespie crossed the finish line of the final stage in Santiago and signalled the end of an extraordinary two weeks of racing. The team's sensational achievement produced a range of emotions among its predominantly injured servicemen members – happiness, relief and joy, but also sadness.

Fourteen incredibly hard stages had seen the guys experience crashes, exclusions, fuelling problems, flooding, altitude sickness, sleep deprivation and broken prosthetics, while driving for up to 18 hours a day in a cramped and hot car, but always aiming for the ultimate goal of seeing the chequered flag in the haze ahead.

'It's not quite sinking in that we've actually done it,' said Matt, his face glowing with heat and happiness, after he'd managed to fight his way through the crowds of fans. 'I'm ecstatic and so proud and pleased for the whole team. Our mechanics and support team kept us in the race and their hard work and dedication were second to none. To complete the Dakar is an incredible achievement in itself, but to become the first ever disability team to cross that finish line lifts the achievement to a whole other level.

'Barney' Gillespie, from Northern Ireland, who is a leg amputee, could hardly find the words to express his elation. 'We have found out first-hand why they call

⬇ Joy sparkles in the Chilean sunlight on her last leg of the record-breaking Dakar 2013

One last time — Matt and
Barney at their final checkpoint

the Dakar the hardest race in the world. It has pushed every single one of us to our limits and beyond. Our team motto is "Beyond injury – achieving the extraordinary" and we've done just that. The support we've received from everyone – our sponsors, supporters, families, friends, the military and complete strangers – has been amazing and is testament to the ability and dedication of this team.'

He went on to say: 'I think the key to our success was actually starting at a slow pace. At the time and during the first week, it wasn't what we wanted as we were always being overtaken and having to drive through the night to make up time, but we adopted the same approach in the second week and it obviously worked! Most vehicles started slowly and then as they settled into the race sped up and were off into the haze – a few hours later we'd see the same car on the side of the road and out of the running. We just said to each other that we've got nothing to prove and we'll carry on doing what we knew worked. We grew a lot closer in those two weeks and we never argued – if the navigator and driver fall out, finishing the Dakar is close to impossible.'

The race began in Peru on 5 January and that was just the start of the team tackling 8,500km of extreme mountain and desert terrain over 15 days. Nothing could have prepared them for the problems and challenges they faced on a nearly hourly basis – the exclusion of Tony Harris and Cathy Derousseaux

← The team gather expectantly for Matt and Barney to bring Joy across the finish line

→ Mission accomplished – Matt and Barney give their first interviews minutes after making Dakar history

⬇ Beyond injury, achieving the extraordinary: a truly miraculous sight, given the previous week's woes, as Joy #445 crosses the line

early on was a massive blow for everyone, as was losing another two cars – but Joy continued to carry the R2R banner and the hopes of all the team, both at home and in South America.

'To be standing in Santiago, knowing we've finished two weeks of this epic journey, feels absolutely brilliant,' said Tony afterwards. It had been a very hard two weeks for both him and Tom, the guys who'd first come up with the idea of Race2Recovery over two years before. Both were eliminated from the race but then focused all their energy on supporting the efforts of Joy.

'Tom and I are obviously disappointed not to finish ourselves, but this project has always been about the team, not the individual.'

Team manager 'Pav' Taylor, was bursting with pride after Joy's finish was confirmed: 'There were times over the past two years, and even two weeks, when this felt like an impossible dream, but here we are and now we can celebrate. One of our biggest aims has been to raise money for Tedworth House. Many of our team members and their families have benefitted from the outstanding recovery process they offer and we hope that our unbelievable experience out here on the Dakar and in the two years beforehand will inspire people to donate.'

'Pav' went on to say: 'I would like to mention Pierre de Frenne, who unfortunately couldn't come out here due to ill health. He supported us right from the beginning and really bought into the spirit of the team; it was such a shame that he missed it but he was in our thoughts every day. I rang him at the finish to say we'd done it and he was over the moon. I know he was devastated not to be out here with us but he's always going to be a big part of the Race2Recovery team and his support and knowledge were invaluable.'

Although the task of packing up the vehicle fleets ready for shipping back to the UK still had to be done, for now the team could just savour the moment when they stood on the famous Dakar podium, heads held high, and enjoyed the glory. And once home, the team would continue celebrating – as well as reconnecting with their families and being in the media spotlight – for some weeks to come, along with enjoying some much-needed sleep in a bed, rather than in a bag on the ground.

STAGE 14
LA SERENA TO SANTIAGO

Road sections	502km
Special stage	128km
Total	630km

Car	Time	Variation	
Joy	2h 36m 55s	52m 45s	77th

← On crossing the line Matt O'Hare and Barney Gillespie took Race2Recovery into the record books as the first disability team to complete the Dakar Rally

↓ A rollercoaster of a ride and team manager 'Pav' Taylor starts to soak it up – the impossible dream has become reality

RACE2RECOVERY
CELEBRATORY PARADE

There are moments in life that we all wish we could bottle and relive again and again. The celebratory parade in Chile was one of these occasions, and for the Race2Recovery team it was one they would never forget.

Thousands of people descended on Santiago, the capital of Chile, to cheer the many finishers but especially the tired old Wildcat, Joy, who still managed to find her legs to take a lap of honour of the city centre before climbing the podium with her crew and support team for a moment that marked the culmination of two years' hard work.

'It's just an incredible feeling,' said Matt O'Hare. 'I drove up on to the podium with half the team sat on the car. Some of the guys were waving their prosthetics in the air to celebrate. A crazy day, but one that makes all the hard work worthwhile.'

⬆ A jubilant Matt
on the podium

⬇ Joyful and triumphant! — waiting for her final trip — the straight run up and over the podium to celebrate

ROYAL CONGRATULATIONS

As if the day couldn't get any better, news came in from the press team that word had spread and even the Royals back in the UK had heard of the team's triumph. The Duke of Cambridge sent a personal message of congratulations to the Race2Recovery team following their historic success in the rally.

'Catherine and I have heard the wonderful news about your success – many, many congratulations.

We know it was not easy but you have become true record holders as the first ever disability team to complete what is one of the world's toughest challenges. What you have achieved was a triumph of perseverance and teamwork, and you have shown the world what true valour looks like. We hope you get some rest now, and, please, no driving like that on our roads when you're back!'

'Barney' Gillespie couldn't stop smiling all day long and said afterwards: 'When I stood on the start line in Lima, all this felt so far away. Then when Joy started overheating and we had to pull over every 30km, it felt even further away. But we made it and it's been great to share this moment with the rest of the team.'

'When Barney and Matt crossed the line, I had a few private words with Barney,' concluded Andrew 'Pav' Taylor, the team manager. 'We're old friends as it was me who first told him about Race2Recovery and introduced him to the lads. I can't remember what I said but I remember welling up when I saw his grinning face knowing that he'd done it. I worked with Barney in 2008 and then met him again at Headley Court when I went outside for a cigarette and saw this guy sitting in a wheelchair with his back to me; we started to chat and the rest, as they say, is history. For him to be the first disabled guy to beat the Dakar is fantastic.'

⬇ Mission accomplished – Race2Recovery proves that having disabilities does not have to stop you realising your dreams

'After I lost my leg, I wanted to do something big to prove to myself and others that anything is still possible, and I've done just that. When we were on the podium, I felt like a huge weight had been lifted.'

Phillip 'Barney' Gillespie

RACE2RECOVERY
EPILOGUE

In the early days, before the funds had been raised and sponsors confirmed, the Race2Recovery fledglings were given some much-needed support and advice from Ben Collins, aka 'The Stig' from BBC TV's *Top Gear*. On hearing what the guys were planning to do, Ben tried to advise them, as he knows only too well, of the dangers of the Dakar...

'When I first met Tony Harris and Pav Taylor from Race2Recovery,' said Ben, 'I felt obliged to try to manage their expectations. The mere thought of severely injured troops catapulting themselves across the dunes of Dakar at over 100mph made me queasy. Crashes at Dakar are nothing short of monumental. Harder still the task of raising the commercial dollars required to foot the bill of competing.'

As we all know now, against the odds, one lone car did cross the line and, at times, it was touch and go. Many motorsport experts, like Ben, were amazed.

'The mixed team of civilian and military personnel, including US Marines, endured all the hellish conditions that South America could throw at them,' stated Ben after the event. 'I still don't fully understand how they did it... Joy, the one successful car, was

↑ A story for Matt and Barney's grandchildren – the Dakar medal, awarded only to the competitors who complete the world's toughest race

special, a cross between a desert flower and a cyborg after all the ad-hoc surgery the team performed to get her to the finish. And finish she did.'

The immediate aftermath of the Dakar Rally was an astonishing and very emotional time for Peter Harrison. The primary purpose of the Peter Harrison Foundation is to support disabled sport and after the death of Peter's wife, Joy, a trustee of the charity, one of the Race2Recovery Wildcats was funded and named in her memory. Peter Harrison founded his charity in 1999 following a serendipitous meeting with Geoff Holt, the renowned disabled sailor and then chairman of Sailability, the charity for disabled sailors. In a similarly serendipitous encounter late in 2012, Paul Bibbey, director of the Peter Harrison Foundation, met Race2Recovery's Matt O'Hare by chance in London and the association between these two charities was born.

Peter, his family, and the team at the Foundation kept up to date with the developments out on the dunes in South America thanks to the team's daily updates. The retirements and never-ending mechanical problems that the team encountered was

read with a sense of intrigue and worry but when Peter heard the incredible news of Joy's success, all he felt was a sense of immense pride. To hear that the car he had funded was the only one to reach the chequered flag seemed like nothing short of a miracle.

'It was an emotional moment for me when I heard of Joy's success as she holds a very special place in my heart,' said Peter. 'Joy was named after my late wife, Joy, who died in September 2012 and I know that if she was here, she would be absolutely delighted. The Peter Harrison Foundation trustees and staff are all very proud and uplifted to have been associated with the Race2Recovery team and its historic and epic success.'

The last word is perhaps best left to the team manager, Andrew 'Pav' Taylor. 'The last 15 days and 5,500 miles has been an incredible journey for everyone – those at home watching and waiting for news and those of us out here, tackling the hostile terrain and finally, going beyond injury and achieving the extraordinary. It has been more intense than any of us could have imagined, but we came through it all together and I'm immensely proud of everyone.'

↖ Jonny Koonja
and Mark Zambon
at the Dakar
Celebratory Parade

↑ Team principal
Quin Evans hitches
a lift to the
podium on Joy

ANDREW 'PAV' TAYLOR

'My job in the team was to deal with problems and manage people – it wasn't easy all the time as I had to be quite mercenary and very much like a strict father figure. Giving up on a problem was never an option, we had to find a solution and that was the end of it.

'I had to be blinkered throughout the whole two weeks and not get caught up in the emotional whirlwind. I had to focus on the day ahead and I took one stage at a time.

On the last night, I thanked them all. To be successful at a world's first is very rare so I couldn't thank them enough. Some had left their jobs to take part and John Winskill even postponed his wedding in order to be part of Race2Recovery; that really is true dedication to the cause.

'It was an honour and a privilege to work with such top-class blokes and it's definitely the hardest thing I've done since being injured. You could compare the tempo of the Dakar to the tempo of operations on the ground at times.'

TONY HARRIS

'Looking back on the Dakar now that I'm home, rested and can see things clearly, I've realised what an eye-opener the whole thing was; right from the early days to the moment we climbed the podium.

'From a personal point of view, I've realised what can be achieved. Together we organised and delivered the Race2Recovery team. Obviously I didn't do it alone – it was a team effort – but in the process I recognised my strong and weak points and just went for it. In the military, everyone has a clear label and is an expert in their field, and you generally have support wherever you turn; in civilian life that support isn't always there.

'After doing Race2Recovery, I have confidence in myself now and know that I can survive life after the military, and not only survive, but really thrive too. This is just the beginning... I hope.'

MATT O'HARE

'The whole team was there to greet us and all I felt was absolute pure elation. I never thought that only one car would finish and I wasn't prepared psychologically for being in the last remaining Race2Recovery car, let alone the only one to finish. I was so sure there would be at least two cars over the line.

'It was just phenomenal and a privilege to stand next to Barney on the podium. We have become really close, as you can imagine, spending two weeks in a very confined space with each other! He was light-hearted and a joy to be around.

'On the fourth night, we were 30km from the end of the special stage. Loads of cars were getting stuck and we had to get out the sand ladders. We worked hard at getting them in place and Barney carried four on his own, with his prosthetic leg, and never made a fuss. It's an honour being able to call him my friend.'

PHILLIP 'BARNEY' GILLESPIE

'It was definitely one of the best days of my life. I was standing on that podium nearly two years to the day after I got blown up.

'Pav did his best to make me cry but I managed to hold it together. He hugged me and I could see in his eyes how he was.

'After I lost my leg, I wanted to do something big to prove to myself and others that anything is still possible, and I've done just that. When we were on the podium, I felt like a huge weight had been lifted. The pressure was there and I think if we hadn't finished, we'd have all come back to the UK with our tails between our legs.

'I'd like to thank my wonderful girlfriend Kirsty, who's been by my side all the way on this unforgettable journey. I'm sure it hasn't been easy, having a boyfriend away a lot and so consumed by Race2Recovery, but I couldn't have done it without her.'

ACKNOWLEDGEMENTS

There are many people who have helped make the Dakar dream come true for everyone at Race2Recovery. There are indeed thousands of you throughout the UK and internationally who have supported the team and our charitable endeavours both emotionally and financially. There are too many to list in person but special thanks must go to:

Cassandra Green, without whom we may never have started. Ed Janvrin and Alex Mackenzie for sowing the seed, and John Hall for never letting us fail. Rory Mackenzie, Neil Heritage, Carl Anstey and Will Dixon for showing us all what could be achieved on Row2Recovery. Trish Chapman, Adam Chapman and Joanna and Eddie Oxnard for believing in us from the start. Lee Bowman for 'getting it' right from the start and opening up his list. Brigadier Ian and the Royal Regiment of Fusiliers family whose support has been constant and unwavering. John Fraser, Elaine and Christine for always making time for us and keeping our spirits up. Mark Elliott for giving us reasons to dream. Dave Falconer for fighting our corner at every turn.

The team at Help for Heroes who do so much for us on behalf of all those who fundraise for them and support us. Stuart Higgins and Jim Williams for their incredible work and support on PR and crisis management. Jim Blackstock for everything he did building us up in the media. Everybody at Keith Gott Land Rovers, especially Morris Booker. Tiff and Debbie for the unglamorous but vital support they gave us along with Camilla, Kiki and John Nicholson, Paul Spackman and Lucy Sykes, Rich Mitchell, Michael Kane and Alexander Harris for your further help with fundraising. Tim, Geoff, Alistair, Adrian, Adam and Simon (aka 'Soundwave') from Gaucho Productions who really became part of the team. Dale Jeffries of Web Print Design Ltd who built and hosted our website (sorry for rolling you over in a Wildcat), we owe a great deal to you for keeping people up to date with the website.

WO1 Stuart Ward, SSgt Andrew Johnston, SSgt David Townend and SSgt Thomas Graham – for providing invaluable help with the preparation of 'The Duff' T5 support truck. Barbara Paterson (aka 'Gran Pat'), thank you for the financial support given to the team enabling us to buy a replacement engine when the old one gave up on our first rally!

And finally, all the team members and their families who sacrificed time at work, income, blood, sweat and God knows what else to make this dream a reality and all our wounded servicemen and women who provide inspiration every time we meet.

Facing page

Clockwise from top: the jubilant Race2Recovery team arrive at Heathrow; a warm welcome from family, friends and fans in a bitterly cold London; Major Matt O'Hare and Corporal Phillip 'Barney' Gillespie with BBC *Top Gear* presenter Richard Hammond; seen with presenters Jeremy Clarkson, Richard Hammond and James May, the team was welcomed back on *Top Gear* after completing the 'impossible' dream; Matt and Barney chat with the media.

This page

From top: Tom Neathway's girlfriend, Rachael Patterson, with her Dakar hero; Baz Whittingham and Lee Townsend can't hide their smiles at being home.

The Race2Recovery Dakar 2013 mission would not
have been possible without the fantastic support
from partner organisations, sponsors and suppliers

BOSCH
Invented for life

QUAIFE

Silverline
4 X 4

GOODRIDGE
FLUID TRANSFER SYSTEMS

norbar
Norbar Torque Tools

SHOWTRAX
INTERNATIONAL

CORBEAU
Professional Motorsport Equipment

LUKE
RACING SYSTEMS

SURF&TURF

INSTANT
SHELTERS

PH
FOUNDATION

Peter Harrison

PLYMOUTH
+ BATTERY CENTRE

DYNAMIC METALS
TITANIUM AND SPECIALIST METALS

XCEED MOTORSPORT.co.uk

GENERAL DYNAMICS
nassco

RALLYEWERK.com
race, rallye and regatta photography
Your race is our office!

GAUCHO PRODUCTIONS

HMS Engineering
(Hereford) Ltd

SUPLEX
GERMANY

LAZER
HIGH PERFORMANCE LIGHTING

Level Peaks
ASSOCIATES

USN
ULTIMATE SPORTS NUTRITION

UBS

3M
PELTOR

N-T-U
NOT FOR THE ORDINARY

inmarsat

alcon
specialist brakes & clutches

Brittany Ferries